Let Me Be Your Servant

100 Reflective Moments

Gene G. Bradbury

BookWilde Children's Books Plus

Let Me Be Your Servant: 100 Reflective Moments

Gene G. Bradbury

ISBN 978-0-9897585-8-1

Printed in the USA by Createspace Independent Publishing Platform.

Book prepress: Kate Weisel, weiselcreative.com

Cover photo by Gene G. Bradbury

All inquiries should be addressed to

BookWilde Children's Books Plus
422 Williamson Rd.
Sequim, WA 98382
genegbradbury.com

Dedication

This book is dedicated to the many parishioners who have shared their lives and stories.

Preface

This book might have been written by any number of care-professionals: rabbi, imam, counselor, or teacher. All have similar experiences. And yet this is about one particular pastor's experiences in parish ministry, college chaplaincy, police chaplaincy, hospital chaplaincy, and prison chaplaincy.

In Norman Maclean's story, *A River Runs Through It*, the father asks the son:

> "You like to tell true stories, don't you?"
>
> "Yes, I like to tell stories that are true."
>
> Then he asked, "After you have finished your true stories sometime, why don't you make up a story and the people to go with it? Only then will you understand what happened and why."

This book is part devotional reading, part memoir, and part reflection. But most of all it is a book of stories that have helped me understand what happened and why. At the same time each reflection invites the reader to re-examine his or her own life. The essays are personal, yet they address issues and questions common to us all.

Some events may remind readers of incidents in their own lives. These stories might have happened anywhere and are reflections on humanity in general. It's a personal journey and reveals much about the writer: what he read, taught, and hopefully learned as a pastor, chaplain, speaker, teacher, youth worker, husband, and father.

I have tried to give credit to the quotations and stories when possible. Where I haven't succeeded, I beg forgiveness.

Last of all, I wish to thank those who have traveled with me: my wife, Debbie, my children and their families. Special thanks to my parents, brothers, sisters, aunts, uncles, and friends. You have all been instrumental in my life. I am also grateful to pastors, teachers, and mentors. And not least, I wish to thank the congregations I've served. You have helped shape my life and my thinking.

May the divine giver enrich your reflections.

Gene G. Bradbury, 2015

Contents

1

Born Barefoot

If we have no peace, it is because we have forgotten that we belong to each other.

Mother Teresa

We begin life barefoot. We need others to bathe us, dress us, and teach us to walk. Our life begins with grace. It's easy to forget that the rest of our life is also dependent on others. No matter how capable we are, we cannot live healthy lives without community.

I don't remember when I first began to wear shoes. How many times did my parents help me put them on? Who taught me to tie my shoelaces? It doesn't matter, of course. What matters is that I learned to tie them and walk on my own. These skills were a gift and remain so in spite of velcro.

The time came when others were not responsible for where I walked. Credit is due them when I chose the right path. But in my meanderings I made some wrong turns. My teachers could not be faulted for that. I'm thankful they were there when I returned like the prodigal son.

As I observe the shoes of others I'm reminded of the old adage: *To understand another you must walk a mile in his shoes.* In these reflections I invite you to walk with me and share my story.

Pause for reflection: Who were my earliest caregivers? Who did I teach to tie their shoes? Who I should thank for my early skills?

2

Starlight Eternity

The night does not come with fruits and flowers and bread and meat;

it comes with stars and stardust, with mystery and nirvana.

John Burroughs

On a clear night the sky seems sprinkled with stars. It is an invitation to marvel. Some say the vastness of the universe diminishes us. Scientists tell us we are made from stardust. Perhaps our value is defined by our participation in the cosmic universe. Chet Raymo, professor of astronomy, writes: . . .*we are flickers of a universal flame — galaxies, stars, planets, life, mind — a seething cauldron of creation. Natural and supernatural, immanent and transcendent, body and spirit will fuse in one God.*

The idea of returning to stardust may not be as comforting as belief in another, heavenly world. It's more comforting, perhaps, to believe we will be reunited with those we love after death. The idea of our return to the stars seems colder and less personal. Yet the idea that I belong to a greater whole has a certain appeal. To know that I am part of a universe billions of years old and will continue among the stars affirms the value of my life now. In some strange way I find it comforting that I will be part of starlight eternity.

Pause for reflection: Can I live with the mystery? How many childhood beliefs have I outgrown? Which matters most, life after death or life now?

3

Behold the Stars

This morning I watched the sky burn, watched matter flowing in the space between the stars. I was up before dawn and I caught in the east the constellations of summer.

Chet Raymo, *The Soul of The Night*

On an autumn night in Oklahoma I wandered into the night and came to a field. I found myself alone with the stars. The wind in the trees seemed to whisper to me.

> Where the asphalt ends
>   blue spruce whispers,
>   "look up, see the stars
>   beholding you."
>
> If all seems dark
>   stars are not lost.
>   Sorrow burns up
>   in their light.
>
> The distant stars
>   invite you to
>   sit at their hearth,
>   warmed by their light.
>
> Behold the stars
> beholding you.

Pause for reflection: When have I experienced life's mystery? What in the natural world speaks most clearly to me? Where do I find it easiest to be still and enjoy?

4

Wilderness Journey

It (the plains) is a radical way of knowing exactly
who, what, and where you are, in defiance of those
powerful forces in society — alcohol, drugs, television,
shopping malls, that aim to make us forget.

Kathleen Norris

Wilderness comes from the Old English which may have come
from *wild-deer-ness.* John Milton refers to it as a place of abundance and
calls it: *a wilderness of sweets.*

Milton's definition catches the rich energy of the wild: the flocks of geese
flying in formation, fish swimming in schools, a herd of horses galloping
across the prairie. What was it like to see thousands of buffalo stamped-
ing across the plains? Wilderness can astonish us.

In the Hebrew Bible *wilderness* was a place of struggle, where the exiles
from Egypt were tested and shaped for the future. It recalled them to reflect on who they were as the a people.

Beethoven experienced wilderness when he became deaf in 1796. Beatrix
Potter entered the wilderness in her extreme loneliness.

I've spent many hours wandering alone. On one occasion my wilderness
was a small space, a phone booth. I was distraught, with nowhere go.
Fortunately, a friend heard the desperation in my voice.

Wilderness experiences can change and enrich our lives. It's often in the
wilderness that we find new direction.

Pause for reflection: When have I felt most alone? How did I
get through the wilderness? What did I learn from it?

5

Sacred Words

Glory be to God for dappled things —
For skies of couple-colour as a brindled cow;
For rose-moles all in stipple upon trout that swim,
Fresh-firecoal chestnut-fals, finches' wings,
Landscape plotted and pieced — fold fallow, and plough;
And all trades, their gear and tackle and trim.

Gerard Manley Hopkins

Looking out the window during worship one Sunday morning my thoughts turned to the mountains. The pastor's words were familiar: *beginning, flesh, glory.* But it was summer. Rivers were flowing. The two-hundred-year-old Douglas fir trees waved in the wind. The religious words seemed old and frail cobwebs. Words about mountains and streams seemed richer, somehow.

Then the pastor's words began to mingle with my thoughts, colliding and bouncing off one another: *Glory of the Lord, gliding bald eagle.* They rolled together: *Word, woods, life, leaves.* Were we thinking about the same thing? The pastor's words were sacred. My thoughts were sacred. The holy was everywhere. I watched the pastor raise her arms to give a blessing like an eagle spreading her wings in benediction.

The word *panENtheism* means God is in everything and everything is in God. It's not the same as *pantheism. PanENtheism* means all exists in God. As Gerard Manley Hopkins suggests, we can give glory to God in all we see, even gear, tackle, and trim.

Pause for reflection: When did I last sit quietly and listen to the natural world? What words speak to me of the sacred? When do I feel closest to the Divine?

Coffee Break

None of us is given life for ourselves alone. We have all come to add what is missing in our world at the moment.

Joan Chittister, OSB

"Come for coffee." It's more than an invitation for a cup of java. The time spent at a kitchen table or local coffee shop is an open door to get to know a person. It says, "I have time for you." The conversation may be about politics, problems at home, work, kids, marriage, or a friend's illness. The topic doesn't matter. What matters is that two people come together. Of course the time is enriched by the aroma of coffee or tea. Call it aroma therapy!

How many cups of coffee have I consumed in homes? Add the number sipped in coffee shops, nursing homes, and hospitals and the number of cups must be in the thousands. No wonder my stomach howls. Yet, the times spent over coffee with another person have been the most productive of my career.

The need for community is part of our human condition. We need those who will listen to us. Perhaps there should be a sign posted over the places where we have coffee that reads: *"There will be friendship served in the coffee room."*

Pause for reflection: Who was the last person I invited for coffee or tea? Who is the friend I turn to when I need someone to listen? Is there someone today who needs a cup of coffee?

Times of Loss

But grief still has to be worked through. It is like walking through water.

Madeleine L'Engle

Grieving for any loss, a person, a job, a divorce, is something we fear and wish to avoid. When loss occurs we want to get though it as quickly as possible. "I can't do this."

It's not uncommon to cover our grief with distractions, hoping it will go away. *Maybe it really didn't happen.* Eventually the pain demands that we face it. Grief cannot be avoided. We must go through it if we are to heal. Grieving is part of the road to wellness. Madeleine L'Engle wrote the words above after her husband's death. Grieving takes time and is painful. We feel as if we are going nowhere."

A man came to me three years after his wife's death. "Shouldn't I be getting over this?" he asked.

"How long were you married?" I asked.

"Sixty years," replied the man.

"Think about that," I said. "You invested sixty years in one another. It's not likely you will get over it in three years. She meant too much to you. She has left an empty spot which you will learn to live with, but you will not get over losing her."

We grieve because we love."

Pause for reflection: What are the losses in my life? How have I managed the grief? Have I used my experience to help another grieving person?

Celebrations

I came that they may have life, and have it abundantly.

John 10:10b

How aware am I of the extraordinary life that passes by each day? In this poem nature called me to pay attention and believe in miracles.

There are Miracles in the Morning

When sun kisses Iowa cornstalks,
red-winged blackbirds tilt their heads
atop fence posts to catch a glint of light.

In Kansas as morning leans fresh
over winter wheat, swelling it like waves,
sunlight dresses the pheasant's plumage.

When Montana's first light passes
along the Blackfoot River, fly-fishermen
cast lines before the kingfisher's eye.

In Washington when eastern sun climbs
Mt. Olympus to paint snow bright,
a blue heron waits perfectly still.

There are miracles in the morning.

Pause for reflection: What do I consider a miracle? When do these miracles occur? Have I shared moments of surprise with someone else?

9

Barely Making It

Out of the depths I cry to you, O Lord,

Lord, hear my voice!

Psalm 130:1

Lucy came to see me on behalf of a friend who had the eating disorder called bulimia nervosa. When she left I made a list of those I knew who were struggling with difficult issues.

In all of these cases I was expected to prayer for them. I also knew problems do not go away without help from others. We can pray for one another; but we also need the help of a friend.

To keep silent and suffer alone is not a good decision.

> An old rabbi asked his pupils how they could tell when the night had ended and the day had begun.
>
> "Could it be," asked one student, "when you can see an animal in the distance and tell whether it's a sheep or a dog?"
>
> "No," answered the rabbi.
>
> Another asked, "Is it when you can look at a tree in the distance and tell whether it is a fig tree or a peach tree?"
>
> "No," answered the rabbi.
>
> "Then how do we tell when day has begun?" the pupils demanded.
>
> "It is when you can look on the face of any man or woman and see that it is your brother or sister; because if you cannot see this, it is still night."

Pause for reflection: When have I experienced hopelessness? Who did I turn to for help? Have I been available to help others who were barely making it?

Flying Solo

*And so Abraham went as the Lord had told him; and
the Lord went with him.*

Genesis 12:4

It takes confidence to do something difficult for the first time. Is a surgeon nervous during her first operation? Is an airline pilot anxious before his first solo flight? How does a child feel entering a new school? Our lives are a series of solo flights.

A great example of confidence is the red knot, a small sandpiper. This courageous bird trusts in its genetic DNA map. The uniqueness of the red knot is its ability to fly long distances. Scientists tell us, "It deserves a reward for the most frequent flyer miles." The red knot leaves the southern tip of South America and flies 10,000 miles to the Canadian arctic to breed. After the young are born the adult birds fly 10,000 miles home. The young birds are left to make the journey on their own. They stop at the same places for food as the adults, never having traveled the route before. Their confidence is built into their genetic makeup.

I remember the first time I entered a hospital emergency room after a death. What was I to offer a woman who had lost her husband? I have had a hundred similar experiences over the years, and each one feels like a solo flight.

Pause for reflection: When do I feel most vulnerable flying solo? How do I handle uncertainty? In what circumstances do I feel uncomfortable?

First Steps

So Jonah set out and went to Nineveh.

Jonah 3:3

How difficult that first step. It wasn't easy for Jonah. It isn't easy for us. To *set out* is an invitation to play the seductive game of "What if." It can stop us in our tracks. "What if I call so and so?" "What if I take this job and not the other?" "What if I don't have the treatment?"

It was the second time the word of the Lord came to Jonah. The first time Jonah ran in the opposite direction and found himself the guest of a great fish. His brain played the game of "What if." "What if I heard it wrong?" "What if the people of Nineveh refuse my message?" We can identify with Jonah and let our head-games confuse us. Jonah needed to hear the message more than once. The second time, he set out for Nineveh to fulfill his calling.

One dark night I walked to an unfamiliar house to meet a family I didn't know. Their fourteen-year-old son had committed suicide. I paused at the door. "What if I say the wrong thing?" "What if their anger turns on me?" What if? What if? What if? The answer is always the same, "Take the first step."

Pause for reflection: What is the hardest decision I've had to make? Did someone help to guide me in that decision? What support can I give to someone who is asking, "what-if?"

12

Who Are You, God? Who am I?

Let us make humankind in our image, according to our likeness; . . .

Genesis 1:26a

The self is a prison of infinite smallness, of minuscule confinement, of suffocating narrowness. It is only by learning to see beyond itself that the self becomes fully alive.

Joan Chittister OSB

There's a story the rabbis tell: "When Adam opened his eyes after creation he did not ask God: *Who are you?* He asked: *Who am I?*"

To ask, *Who are you, God?* is like the beetle asking the gardener who she is. "This is my world, my dirt." The finite cannot realistically address the infinite. To understand the divine we must begin with ourselves.

I called on Jason in the hospital. He'd attempted to take his own life more than once. It was obvious Jason didn't like himself. This hatred confused his understanding of his world, his friends, his parents, and himself. He wanted rid of himself. Jason couldn't accept the fact that others valued him.

The scriptures from various traditions instill value in their readers by affirming the divine spirit within them. This is where I must begin by knowing that I have value within me. When I understand that I can move out into the universe. Only then am I able to love myself and others.

Pause for reflection: When do I feel most valued? What does it mean to be spiritual person? How does my sense of being valued affect how I see others?

Living With Weeds

Murphy's Law: *"If anything can go wrong, it will."*

O'Tool's Commentary on Murphy's Law: *"Murphy was an optimist."*

A book by E. L. James, *Fifty Shades of Gray* is about compromise, choices, and betrayal. The title, *Shades of Gray,* recalls a world without definite color. Decisions are not black and white, but gray. Too often we must navigate murky waters. Should I tell someone if I know a friend is being abused? Should I be honest with a person about his excessive drinking? Choices are often hard, made difficult because the answers are difficult.

We live with weeds. "Should I pull the weeds or let them grow?" asks the servant in Jesus' parable. I will always live with gray areas and know there are consequences to my choices. What will the result be if I make this decision instead of that one? Will it hurt someone? Is it safe? Living with unclear answers may require talking with someone I can trust. I may need to confide in someone who has lived with weeds and wrestled with tough decisions.

I've spent time in dark places asking, "What should I do?" The answer has seldom been back or white. Yet after quiet contemplation I have been able to move forward and live with shades of grey.

Pause for reflection: What decisions have I resolved unwisely? What decisions in my past proved to be the right ones? How do my past decisions, right or wrong, help me to help others?

The Other Voice in My Head

But this was very displeasing to Jonah,
and he became angry.

Jonah 4:1

Poor Jonah, he's like a child pouting under the kitchen table because he was told, "No!"

"Lord God, I did everything you asked and look what happened. You should have punished the people of Nineveh." In frustration Jonah builds a booth and sits down to die.

It's easy to assume that God is on my side. "Why doesn't my neighbor clean up his yard?" "Why doesn't that mother take the crying child out of church?" How easy it is to condemn entire ethnic groups I don't understand.

Jonah, eager to judge the people of Nineveh, assumed God felt the same as he did. I, too can be parochial in my thinking. I can even support my thinking with religious conviction.

As a young man I sat in a pastor's office and heard him give me helpful advice. His was a voice of caring and reason. My own stubborn voice was already made up. I did not listen.

Jonah, his feelings hurt, turns in on himself. His world becomes small and he cannot see the larger picture. How hard it is to listen to the other voice that asks us to do the right thing.

Pause for reflection: When have I been too quick to judge another person? How might I become more accepting of others? Am I willing to invest the time it takes to get to know the person I don't understand?

15

Ashes in Springtime

Ashes, ashes, all fall down.

Children's nursery rhyme

The season of Lent is observed by many churches in early spring. It begins on Ash Wednesday with the imposition of ashes on the forehead as a sign of penitence. The spirit of the season comes close to the Jewish Day of Atonement. Ashes in the Jewish and Christian traditions remind worshippers of their mortality and need of forgiveness.

There is another meaning in the use of ashes, one that focuses on renewal. The word *Lent* comes from the Anglo-Saxon word meaning *springtime.* It's a time of personal renewal. Farmers burn their fields to prepare them for planting. Fire burns off the old and renews the soil.

In this understanding spring is a season of fresh beginnings . Think of ashes not as a public display of self-righteousness as warned against in Matthew's gospel. Rather see ashes as a sign of personal growth. In the dark months of winter I anxiously look at flower catalogues and gardening books. I long for the warmth of spring and signs of new birth. Ashes turn my thoughts to *spiritual springtime.* Ash Wednesday is an invitation to look for spring in myself. Following the dark months of winter, I yearn for spring fields and renewal of my inner spirit.

Pause for reflection: Are my worship practices used in a positive way? How might I practice springtime and nurture my own spirit? What are my personal spring celebrations?

Vitality

*How beautifully the leaves grow old! How full of light
and color are their last days!*

John Burroughs, *Under the Maples*

John Burroughs, writer and naturalist, at the end of his life spoke
of his love for the maple tree when he wrote the words above. Surely he
was thinking of his later years. I've seen the same light and color in others as they grow older. I envy them and hope my last years are as full of
life as theirs.

My friend and mentor, Mrs. Storvick, was full of life and color. I didn't
see that when I was a teenager. She seemed always in our way. We weren't
always kind to her. Yet she was always gracious. Mrs. Storvick possessed
so much energy that many saw her as a nuisance. Only in later years did
I understand her enthusiasm and vitality. Her joy came from within. It
wasn't artificial, placed there for others to see and admire. Her vitality
came from an inside source. She loved life and naturally wished to share
it with others.

I came to recognize that Mrs. Storvick possessed a great faith. Like the
maple tree in autumn she shone forth in yellow and bronze, lighting up
all who came near. She was a beautiful person in her autumn years.

Pause for reflection: Where does my greatest joy come from?
Do others see vitality and joy in me? Who do I know that expresses this
special gift?

The Garden of Dilemma

Then the eyes of both were opened, . . .

Genesis 2:7a

How did all the trouble begin? Why evil? Why do we make bad choices? To live is to make choices: to eat or not to eat; to go or to stay; to tell or not tell; to act or not act. The garden can be a blessing and a curse.

As infants our choices were made for us. Our eyes were not yet open to responsibility. Like Adam and Eve standing under the tree of knowledge, we were told what was best for us. That didn't stop us from asking questions: "How do I know it's true?" "Shouldn't I be able to make my own decisions?"

One day in my exasperation with a young confirmation student who always arrived late, I lost my good judgment. I reprimanded her in front of the class. She ran home to her grandmother in tears. The phone call came shortly after class. I apologized, but the damage was done. Living in the Garden of Dilemma is to be human.

It's risky standing below the tree and looking at those bright red apples. Should I or shouldn't I? We may know the answer, but it's only when the final decision is made that our eyes are opened and we know if the choice was good or bad.

Pause for reflection: What choices have I made that hurt others? How did my mistakes change me? Did they help me make more responsible decisions later?

18

Change Your Bumper Sticker

I have desired to go
Where springs not fail,
To fields where flies no sharp and sided hail
And a few lilies blow.

And I have asked to be
Where no storms come,
Where the green swell is in the havens dumb,
And out of the swing of the sea.

Gerard Manley Hopkins, *Heaven-Haven*

When I fail and feel guilty there is nothing I'd rather do than disappear like Alice down the rabbit hole.

A young women tapped on my office door, a small bird with ruffled feathers. "I feel so guilty," she said. "I go to church, but I can't feel forgiven."

Many today live in a heaven and hell framework with a feeling of judgment and condemnation. If the bumper sticker on your car reads, "Guilty," it may be time to change that bumper sticker.

Where can I find a heaven-haven? Finding such a place may mean knocking on a friend's door. It may be time to sit quietly somewhere and put things in perspective. When the storm rages, like a ruffled bird I must look for a safe branch to weather out the storm. I have been fortunate in my life to have people I can turn to in times of desperation. They have helped me see that my bumper sticker needs changing.

Pause for reflection: When have I felt most like a failure? Who did I find to talk to? Have I been able to let my past failures go?

The Free Gift

But the free gift is not like the trespass.

Romans 5:15a

I've been the recipient of many gifts through the years. Congregations have been generous in saying goodbye and thank you when I've left a parish. I'm always surprised by the number of people who turn out to wish my family well. On our bed is a quilt made by congregation members as a reminder of our time together.

How hard it is for us to accept gifts. The Apostle Paul wrote about such a gift. He wanted to make it clear that the Law brings judgment. Then he counters the Law by pouring grace like sweet syrup over the whole mess. Loved by God I need not live under judgment. The free gift is the certain announcement of our acceptance.

How is it unlike the Law? The answer is: grace is not up to me. The very nature of grace is that it's a given. I can't muck it up no matter how hard I try. The gift is an absolute assurance that I'm loved. I can make it more difficult by trying to find a way to win God's love. But it isn't necessary. The love of God is already mine.

Pause for reflection: Who are those who have spoken words of grace to me? When did I last speak a word of grace to another person? Am I able to simply say thank you when a gift is given?

Surviving

It's not difficult to become smart. It is difficult to become enlightened enough to be able to distinguish what is smart from what is wise.

Joan Chittister

It's a familiar encounter: "command these stones to become loaves of bread;" "throw yourself down;" and "All these I will give you." Matthew places this story of the temptation immediately after Jesus' baptism.

The wilderness becomes a place of preparation for what lies ahead. The years in the wilderness prepared the Israelites to enter the Promised Land. Jesus entered the wilderness before his ministry began. Would he be up to the task? The tempter does his best to redirect Jesus' purpose. But Jesus would not be side-tracked.

I remember one period in my ministry when I experienced deep depression. Curled up in a fetal position I entered the wilderness, lost and alone. It was time to seek help during a period of uncertainty. Uncertainty can keep us from moving ahead. Are my personal needs and wants distracting me from what I have to do? If they are it's time to seek advice that will move me from a fetal position to one of health.

The wilderness metaphor is a call to evaluate one's self. It's a time to answer hard questions. Desert experiences often prepare us for what is to come.

Pause for reflection: How do I view periods of depression and boredom? Do dry periods bring me new understanding? How might I use wilderness experiences in a healthy way?

21

Expecting the Worst, Receiving the Best

He will again have compassion upon us; .. . .

Micah 7:19a

As a young teenager I took myself too seriously. When the pastor's wife of our congregation suggested changes in the youth program, I took affront. As president I suggested we write a letter asking her to let us run our own program. I know she was hurt by this. But she was a caring person and backed away graciously. She did not judge us, but treated us with love as she always did.

The prophet Micah saw something missing in the worship practices of Judah. He put Judah on trial before God. Judah had applied itself to worship and sacrifice, but had not served God. Should they have offered more sacrifice? It was not more showy worship or sacrifice that God required, but his people to do justice in serving others.

When Judah's trial was over a surprise verdict awaited them. The people of Judah had been found wanting; but instead of condemnation, they received pardon. "Who is a God like you, pardoning iniquity and passing over the transgression."

When we fail we look for the axe to fall. Judah found a just judge who pardoned and called them to practice authentic worship in serving others. Expecting the worst, they received the best.

Pause for reflection: Have I given back the grace I've received? Have I denied justice to another person? Have I surprised anyone with compassion when anger was expected?

Listen to Your Heart

One shouldn't be too upset about the way the ball bounces if one has dropped it oneself.

William Sloane Coffin

Second Isaiah, chapters 40-55, was written toward the end of Judah's exile in Babylon. It reflects the despair of those who returned to Jerusalem. Expecting to be welcomed, they were disappointed. Isaiah wrote to lift the hearts of those who returned and to focus their attention on future goals. In Babylon they learned what it was to be suffering servants. Would this knowledge be used to bring new life to the world?

I've had many Isaiah's in my life, those who have picked me up when I've despaired. These friends and mentors helped me survive the desert experiences. They filled me with hope when I was hopeless. It raises the same question God must have asked the people of Judah: Will you who know what it is to despair become messengers of hope? Will you use your new understanding to reach others?

Isaiah 51 sounds the trumpet: "Listen to me, Listen to me, Awake, Awake." Go and give hope to those who have no hope. Second Isaiah is quick to point out that those who have experienced God's righteousness are best equipped to help others who are searching for reassurance.

Pause for reflection: Has my own despair enabled me to be more compassionate with others? Have I become less judgmental? Have I been able to leave behind my past periods of exile?

23

Over-Flowing Fountains

Or is God the God of Jews only? Is he not God of the Gentiles also?

Romans 3:29

How often I limit God's grace to those like myself. The Apostle Paul was overwhelmed by God's love. That experience helped him discover an important truth. Grace was for all people. It was not to be offered drip by drip, but as an over-flowing fountain.

Paul reveled in God's unconditional love. He must have danced when he learned that his acceptance did not depend upon him. As a result he found it impossible to restrict grace to those unlike himself. Grace was to be shared abundantly.

We have all experienced grace moments when we have been given a unexpected gifts. These were cause for joyful celebrations. But grace extended is not always accepted. I invited a pastor from a different tradition to lunch. "I'm sorry, we do not fellowship with those of other denominations," he said. He was operating from a defensive, protective position. "We have the truth and must guard it from contamination."

I prefer the response where God's grace is celebrated. We have received grace. Isn't it best to offer grace to others?

Pause for reflection: Have I been stingy with God's love? Has my prejudice or dislike created a barrier between myself and others? When have I been able to overlook the differences in another person and offer grace instead?

Mixed Baggage

I will bless those who bless you, and the one who curses you I will curse . . .

Genesis 12:3

Abraham lived in a time of blessings and curses. Every god brought potential good or evil. Abraham packed his bags with the understanding of both and left home. His faith and obedience made him the father of three major world religions: Judaism, Christianity, and Islam. Each tradition has been guilty of both blessings and curses.

We no longer live in a world where gods threaten to curse us. Unfortunately we leave that to one another. It is easy to pack our bags with curses and unkind thoughts. What is needed today are those who pack their bags with blessings. Blessings are lighter and easier to carry. They are also more fun to unpack. When I'm blessed or have been a blessing, I sleep well. This is never true after carrying curses in my luggage.

One day I received a letter with five hundred dollars enclosed. More important than the money was the note that came with the gift. It was from a couple for whom I waved the marriage honorarium twenty-five years before. Perhaps it was a blessing to them at the time. They remembered the incident twenty-five years later. I was blessed.

Pause for reflection: Have I found it easy to be drawn into negative talk about others? Who has been a blessing to me? When have I been a blessing to others?

Coming and Going

The Lord will keep your going out and your coming in . . .

Psalm 121: 8

Entering an observant Jewish home you may find a Mezuzah on the door post. The small box contains the Schema: "Hear, O Israel: The Lord is our God, the Lord alone..." (Deut. 6:9) Psalm 121 parallels the practice from Deuteronomy: ". . . and write them on the doorposts of your house and on your gates."

The sacred is not only present to us in worship or prayer, but at all times. The Jews believed God is there at our birth and death. The teaching is reflected in daily life. God is present as we pass through the door on the way to work or school. God is there when we return home in the evening. The Mezuzah reminds the Jews of God's intimacy.

What a comfort to know we're not alone. God is that accompanying shadow as we walk down the street. Like Tevye in *Fiddler on the Roof*, I find myself in conversation with the sacred. I need not wait for certain moments to pray. Doors and gates are good reminders of God's abiding presence. Walking along the wheat fields in Kansas on Sunday morning before worship, I fell into conversation with the divine.

Pause for reflection: What things distract me from the Divine presence? How often during the day do I pause to listen? How might I pay better attention to God's abiding presence?

Open Arms

Abraham believed God, and it was reckoned to him as righteousness.

Romans 4:3

The Apostle Paul was fond of talking about Law and Gospel, a topic I often find muddled and difficult to understand. The key to making sense of Law and Gospel is to begin with God rather than myself. If I begin with the knowledge that God is the actor in our relationship and acts on my behalf, it becomes "good news."

It's simple when I understand that I am loved because of who God is. God is love. I am not loved because I deserve love. I am like the child welcomed onto the mother's lap because she is who she is. There are no conditions. It's as simple as that.

My part becomes easy: I simply trust and run into the arms of God's presence. There's are no Rules standing in the way. Why is this so hard for us to grasp? Perhaps it's because as adults we're not used to unconditional acceptance.

I remember one professor who was busy when I knocked on his door. I'm certain it was an interruption; but he rose from his desk and said, "It is so good to see you." It's something I've never forgotten. It was a genuine welcome, always a great gift.

Pause for reflection: When was the last time I received an unconditional welcome? How did I feel? When was the last time I welcomed another person unconditionally?

Night Questions

The theory of a thing is so much easier than the practice. The theory is in the air, the practice is in the woods; the eye, the thought, travels easily where the foot halts and stumbles.

John Burroughs

The Gospel of John differs from the other gospels in its emphasis on *believing*. John uses the word *believe* or its equivalent ninety times. Matthew, Mark, and Luke use it only a few times. It's no surprise that those who focus on belief prefer John's gospel.

John wrote before the early church established its doctrinal position. The followers of Jesus were still trying to explain who he was. There were various opinions. Nicodemus represents this period of questioning. What was Nicodemus looking for when he came by night? It's unlikely he was expecting to hear that Jesus was the Son of God. In this night-time conversation Jesus invited Nicodemus to think about his own relationship with God.

Driving to the hospital at 2:00 a.m. in the Texas sweltering heat, I thought of Nicodemus. A man had died. His widow waited with questions. What was I to say to her? Her life would never be the same. Night questions draw us into deeper conversations where God is present.

Pause for reflection: How much of my life is based on *belief* rather than *practice*? Do I judge others by what they believe or by how they live? How much is required to believe and what is required to practice one's faith?

Listening to the Silence

Let the preacher tell them the truth. Before the Gospel is a word. It is silence. It is the silence of their own lives and of his life. It is life with the sound turned off . . .

Frederick Buechner

Like the people of Israel before him Jesus, entered the desert. In the silence he heard his own voice and the voice of the enemy. He was tempted by the voice of enticement and distraction.

Outside voices can be very persuasive. "What do you really want?" "You may only get this one chance." "Why shouldn't you have what makes you happy?" In my early life I listened to other voices rather than to the voice of reason.

"Before you go through a divorce at least see a counselor." This was the clear and wise voice of reason. I chose instead to hear my own voice, a voice already made up. We all wrestle with alternative voices. I chose to follow the wrong voice and others were hurt. I was unwilling to listen.

Where there is loss there is often gain. From my experience I learned how to listen more to the silence. It is often there that the Spirit comes and brings comfort and direction.

Pause for reflection: Who in my past spoke in a clear and wise voice when I needed one? Under what circumstances have I ignored the voice of reason? What have I learned from the voices in my past?

A Golden Bird to Sing

Ah, those mornings when you are awakened by the singing, the matins of the birds!

Henry David Thoreau

A golden bird in William Butler Yeats' poem sang of what was past, what was passing, and what was to come, and so interested a drowsy emperor.

The task of prophets, poets, and artists is to wake us up. John the Baptist was such a voice, singing in the wilderness of what was past, what was passing, and what was to come. I'm thankful for the pastor who called me into his office when I was a teenager. "How would you like to go to college?" he asked. He was thinking about my past, present, and future.

The painter Van Gogh had a vision of humanity as a marvelous creation in which the world of eternity meets the world of time and space. His painter's eye gave him patience to see eternity in the humblest peasant. He painted human flesh as a sanctuary of sacred energy.

How sleepy I can be. I need a golden bird to sing and wake me up: to help me learn from the past, alert me to what is passing, and help me stay awake for what is to come. My drowsiness can cause me to miss so much of the natural world and the wonderful nuances of life.

Pause for reflection: Have I missed a special moment today? What was said to me in passing? How might I pay more attention to the details?

A Lyrical Event

We are haunted by our yearning to be addressed . . .

Walter Brueggemann

Sacred scriptures from all traditions provide us with lyrical poetry. Too often we try to literalize the words or over-interpret their meaning. Much of sacred scripture is written to be read aloud or sung. Like fine wine or good food, one must take time to taste and savor.

There are beautiful words from less familiar traditions that can enrich our lives. One of my favorites is this verse from the Navajo Way Prayer:

In beauty all day long, may I walk.

Through the returning seasons, may I walk.

On the trail marked with pollen, may I walk.

With dew about my feet, may I walk.

To reframe Walter Bruggemann's words about preaching, our language must carry a lyrical meaning that breaks the muteness and shatters the deathly control in which our lives are held. Reading sacred scripture and poetry invites us to slow down and pay attention to the rhythms of our lives. It's an invitation to hear the deeper meaning. Let the words break into the mundane periods of our lives. Read slowly. Listen, rather than read for information or to complete a page. Let the music sing.

Pause for reflection: When did I last read beautiful words and really listen? Do I let my reading for information get in the way of beautiful writing? What book in my home is like an old friend that I enjoy again and again?

Letting Go

Albert Brewster

Aged 25 years

Killed by a falling tree

What was important to Albert Brewster? He died long ago according the grave marker. The longer I live the more I realize life is about letting go as much as it is about holding on. We begin as infants by losing our baby fat. I wasn't so happy when I began losing my hair and my eyesight changed. I was surprised one day to find I was no longer young.

I was unprepared to let go of someone close to me. When my younger sister died in a car accident it took me a long time to realize I had to let her go. I have talked with people in assisted living who find it difficult to let go of their independence. Eventually I, too, will have to depend more and more on others. Like Albert Brewster, I will finally let go of life itself.

"Do not store up for yourselves treasures on earth, where moth and rust consume and where thieves break in and steal," said Rabbi Jesus. We want to hold onto things and those we love. The reality of letting go should cause us to appreciate what we still hold onto today.

Pause for reflection: What has been the hardest thing I've had to let go? Do I take the time to appreciate what I have and the people I know? How might I prepare for the end of life?

Letting Go, Part II

Sometimes the smallest experience helps us see life in unexpected ways. So it was when a hummingbird fell from the bird feeder on a very cold day. He seemed a small prophet heralding a message of new life.

To Rise Again

He swooned backwards
from the bird-feeder,
falling, wings folded
on wet autumn leaves.

If death is like that,
it's beautiful, the color of
folded hummingbird wings,
silent and soft.

The tiny heart beat slowly,
turned over, hugging loam,
absorbing morning sun
warmth from mother earth.

Awakened, redeemed, flying,
small heart no longer weak,
unwilling to let the day begin
without a humming-bird song.

Pause for reflection: How often do I pass by the small pleasures in life because I am looking for more? What small but meaningful encounter did I have today? How might I train myself to pay more attention?

33

Contagious Peace

The soul is the sense of something higher than ourselves,
something that stirs in us thoughts, hopes, and
aspirations which go out to the world of goodness,
truth, and beauty.

Albert Schweitzer

The monk who did everything and the monk who did nothing are the same St. Benedict dedicated himself to God and established a spiritual practice while he lived. After his death when he himself could do nothing himself, his spiritual practice still remained.

St. Benedict lived as a hermit in a cave after leaving Rome. His years in the cave prepared him inwardly and gave him peace. He found the peace needed to spend the rest of his life serving others. Even after his death, so the story goes, the cave retained enough of Benedict's peace of soul to have a healing effect on those who came to visit.

There are those whose very presence seems to have an inner peace that heals. I have known such people. What is it that lingers even after they have left the room? Have they found peace in themselves and are at home in their own skin? To be in their presence is like being warmed at a hearth fire. To use another metaphor, they are the fragrant perfume that lingers even in their absence.

Pause for reflection: When do I experience peace in myself? Who do I know that exemplifies genuine peace? Am I comfortable enough in myself that I am able to convey peace to others?

A Lantern on the Road

If one is to do good, it must be done in minute particulars.

William Blake

How important is it to be welcomed with genuine warmth into someone's home? To have someone greet us is to know we are valued. To come home to a cold house with no one present leaves an empty feeling. How many children experience this kind of homecoming after school? 1 How many arrive at an airport to find no one waiting?

Beth Streeter Aldrich in her novel, *A Lantern in Her Hand*, tells of a pioneer woman who leads the way for her family through the rigors of pioneer life. She's the one who meets them on the road as they come home in the dark. She's there, a lantern in her hand, at the end of the day.

This willingness to trim the lamp and be there is a particular gift. Wherever we are, a sincere and friendly welcome lifts us to new heights. It reminds us that we are worth a special effort. Rabbi Harold Kushner in his book, *Living a Life that Matters*, suggests that we all need to be valued, ". . .not because of our achievements, but because we are loved by God and loved by the people around us."

Pause for reflection: Who made a special effort to welcome me? What was it like to come home after school as s child? What traditions of welcome did my family practice?

35

Hospitality

Hospitality is one form of worship.

Jewish Proverb

I was invited to consider a job in a small town in eastern Washington State. The wheat fields were truly *golden waves of grain.* The people were pleasant. One particular thing impressed me more than any other. Our daughter was elementary school age and we were invited to see the school. The principle met us at the door to welcome us. The smell of freshly baked bread was obvious as we entered the hallway. I asked about this. The principle's response was:

"The school cafeteria makes bread every day. We want the children to feel at home. There's nothing more comforting than the smell of freshly baked bread."

There is a Gaelic Rune that expresses the gift of hospitality:

> I saw a stranger yesterday:
> I put food in the eating place,
> Drink in the drinking place,
> Music in the listening place;
> In the blessed name of the Triune
> He blessed myself and my house,
> My cattle and my dear ones,
> And the lark said in her song
> Often, often, often
> Goes the Christ in the stranger's guise.

Hospitality is a vital part of all religious traditions. We know it in many forms: a warm hug, a welcoming smile, and the smell of warm bread from the oven.

Pause for reflection: When have I been generous in giving hospitality? How might I become more hospitable? Have I been welcomed warmly when I did not expect it?

The Secret Garden

When Mary Lennox was sent to Misselthwaite Manor to live with her uncle everybody said she was the most disagreeable-looking child every seen.

Francis Hodgson Burnett, *The Secret Garden*

The Secret Garden by Frances Hodgson Burnett tells the story of Mary, a young girl orphaned by the death of her parents in India. She's sent to live with her uncle who grieves the loss of his young wife. Mary seeks love and acceptance only to find an uncle who avoids her. Then Mary discovers a secret garden locked away by her uncle. A world of beauty and acceptance is opened to her.

Provide a child with an atmosphere of love, and acceptance and she will thrive. But, it is easy for adults to lock doors that keep a child out. I received a call from a distraught mother who confided in me that her eighth grade daughter told her she did not believe in God. She was shocked by her daughter's confession. "I would never neglect my children's secular education. But I have neglected their religious education. What can I do?"

The incident is a reminder of how easy we fail to open certain doors for our children. Doors need to be opened at the right time When that happens, our children surprise us.

Pause for reflection: Did I experience locked doors in my childhood? What doors were opened to me as a child? Whose hand do I remember holding as a child?

Is Anybody Listening?

Life being what it is, if we don't make a difference by trying, we'll make a difference by not trying.

William Sloane Coffin

After retirement from full-time parish ministry I returned to school to get a degree in spiritual direction. In the sessions of supervised spiritual direction with directees, I was told I must learn to listen more carefully. I had listened for years to people in homes, hospitals, nursing homes, and in my office. But had I listened deeply?

Too often pastors find themselves in the role of counselor and want to fix a problem. Soon we realize that we can give support but cannot always fix things. Spiritual direction moves beyond counseling by providing intense empathic listening. For pastors used to talking it's more difficult to sit and listen. We need those who can listen and walk with us in our thoughts. A truly good listener enables us to think things through and help ourselves.

Spiritual directors do not have answers to give in these situations. They cannot fix a person's problem. They give of themselves in concentrated time. A spiritual director offers a quiet calming presence when a good listener is needed. In moments of quiet when we know someone is walking with us in our thoughts, healing becomes possible.

Pause for reflection: Do I know someone who needs a good listener? When was the last time I needed someone to listen? Who was the last person to really listen to me?

Vultures on the Windowsill

We have only what we cannot lose in a shipwreck.

Sufi saying

Roy and Sharon lived in a small house with two toddlers. Problems seemed to roost on their windowsill. They had little money. The children were often sick. Sharon was worn out from her job and shuffling the kids to Grandma's house. Both parents were tired and depressed. They stared out the window at a gray and hopeless life.

The night Roy told his wife about losing his job, the refrigerator broke down. Sharon packed up the kids and moved to her mother's house. Roy and Sharon weren't bad people, but their lives were in chaos. The vultures sitting on the windowsill waited to do their worst.

I experienced this sense of failure when I first moved to Washington state. I wasn't making a good salary and was late with a car payment. The knock at the door was from a man who came to repossess our only automobile. As it happened, friends were visiting our home and offered to help. Where does one turn when trouble knocks on the door?

A pastor and his wife heard of Roy's and Sharon's situation. Anonymously, they bought a used appliance and had it delivered. The family didn't belong to the pastor's church. They were simply neighbors who needed help at a difficult time.

Pause for reflection: When did I last feel hopeless? Was there anyone there to help? When did I last help someone who was desperate?

Wrinkles in Time

It was a dark and stormy night. In her attic bedroom
Margaret Murray, wrapped in an old patchwork
quilt, sat on her bed and watched the trees tossing in
the frenzied lashing of the wind.

Madeline L'Engle, *A Wrinkle in Time*

AS I listen to poetry, story, and parable I hear below the surface writing. With the first notes of Madeline L'Engle's story, I know something is about to happen. Stories and parables express a universal truth. Perhaps this is why we, like Jesus, use them so often.

The opening line of a story invites me inside. The first paragraph is designed to grab my attention. If I were to write my own story what would the first line be? How would I begin? How would I grab the reader's attention? Here are a few first-liners:

"It was the best of times, it was the worst of times."
Charles Dickens, *A Tale of Two Cities.*

"Call me Ishmael." Herman Melville, *Moby Dick.*

"Mrs. Dalloway said she would buy the flowers herself."
Virginia Woolf, *Mrs. Dalloway.*

"Twas the night before Christmas, when all through the house . . ." Clement Clarke Moore, *The Night Before Christmas.*

"The moving was over and done."

Willa Cather, *The Professor's House.*

My life story should begin with a great first line like . . .

Pause for reflection: What is my story? What would my story say about what I believe? What would my story say about my character?

40

The Star Thrower

Life is cooperation with other lives. We win when we help others win.

John Burroughs

A book that greatly influenced me was Loren Eiseley's collection of essays entitled *The Star Thrower*.

Loren Eiseley, an anthropology, professor tells of his walk on the beaches of Costabel. In the distance he sees a figure stooping to pick something from the sand. As he approaches he sees a man retrieving starfish that have washed ashore. The man is throwing the starfish back into the sea. Inquiring the reason for this, the man says, "I'm throwing the stars into the sea that they might live again."

It's a wonderful image. It's what pastors, doctors, nurses, teachers, and public servants do. It is what we should all be about. It should be true of our relationship to the earth and all the creatures on the earth. It should be our task in relation to one another. Shouldn't we all be picking up lives that are abandoned and broken that they might be restored to places where life is possible?

We cannot always restore life. But each of us can lend a hand to those who have fallen or been washed ashore. I'm thankful for those who have stooped to help me when I needed it most. Sometimes they have been strangers. At other times they have been family and friends.

Pause for reflection: Have I thrown back any starfish lately? Where are they now? When have I been a star-thrower?

41

Tears Like Rain

I've often been called to a place of crisis: a death, family crisis, a suicide. None of us are exempt from tragedy, illness, and pain. But we hope that when it comes to us, there will be others there to see us through.

> I will stand in rain
> under dark skies,
> gather the tears
> of those far away;
> feel their wet-weeping
> run down my face,
> for who can deny
> that we, like they,
> live under like sky.
>
> When in suffering
> my own tears are shed,
> I'll look to the clouds
> passing high overhead,
> let my weeping
> be carried aloft
> to drop like rain
> on those far off,
> who share like pain.

Pause for reflection: How does the suffering of others affect me? Who has seen me through dark days? In what way does suffering with another person affect our relationship?

42

Flaws

Flaws and inadequacies come with the territory of being human.

Joyce Rupp

How hard it is for us to make sense of our faults. To be human is to fail as well as to succeed. In her book, *The Cup of Our Life,* Joyce Rupp tells of a friend who owned a beautiful bowl with a crack in it. Her friend turned the crack to the wall so that no one would see it. Haven't we all done that?

How many times have I turned my imperfections to the wall? I hope I've learned from these experiences. I once listened to gossip about a colleague. I should have suggested to the person complaining that he go and talk to my colleague directly. I didn't and therefore gave the impression that I agreed with the complaint. When my colleague heard of this, she confronted me. My reaction was defensive and angry. Then I realized she was right. I apologized. It was a valuable lesson I would not have learned without the mistake and her courage to confront me.

Flaws come with being human. At times we can spend too much time dwelling on our imperfections. It's best to call them by name and use them in understanding ourselves. Perhaps the vase is still in place, crack and all, because it is still useful.

Pause for reflection: What have been my greatest mistakes? Did I learn from them? How have my failures helped me to understand others?

43

My Shadow, My Friend

Making friends with your shadow helps facilitate your acceptance of yourself as a less-than-perfect human being. We have a dark side; we are not all light.

William Miller

I don't find it easy to live with my shadows. They seem to hang around the umbrella stand waiting for me to open the door. As I leave the house, they follow me through the day.

Sometimes it's the impatient shadow or the quick-to-anger shadow. There is the accusing shadow, the self-pity shadow, and others I need not name. You get the idea. Shadows are sneaky. They duck in and out of days. They disappear in the light. Making friends with them is to acknowledge that they are real. Only then can I control them and learn from them.

It's not enough to deny my impatience. I need to look deeper and ask why I'm impatient. Why can't I allow that person to do it their way? Why am I in such a hurry? Why do I place so much importance on what people think?

As we get older our shadows become our friends. They're here to stay; why not get to understand them? Now as I leave the house, I look at the umbrella stand and invite one of these shadows along. "Come, we'll see how it goes today. But remember, I'm in control, not you."

Pause for reflection: What are the current shadows in my life? How am I dealing with them? Have I developed any new shadows?

44

Sublime Sight

*Only the wondering eye sees the sacred horizon
enfolded within the petals of a blue flower.*

Sam Keen

Our daughter was eight years old and collected everything from sea shells to bird's nests. What a thrill it was for her to pick up a piece of rock and discover a leaf fossil millions of years old. It was one among many discoveries we encouraged as parents. Our outings were often to the zoo, museum, or a walk along an estuary.

Jesus' parable of the buried treasure reminds me of these times.

> The Kingdom of heaven is like a treasure hidden in a field
> which someone found and hid; then in his joy he goes and
> sells all that he has and buys that field.

It's a wonderful feeling when we discover something for ourselves. The words of Abraham Heschel, the great Jewish teacher, come to mind:

> "But there is no education for the sublime. We teach the
> children how to measure, how to weigh. We fail to teach
> them how to revere, how to sense wonder and awe . . . yet
> without it, the world becomes flat and the soul a vacuum."

If we give nothing else than the gift of wonder to another person, we will have done enough.

Pause for reflection: When did I first feel the joy of discovery? Who contributed to my longing to discover? How have I helped children to discover wonder in their world?

45

On the Outside

Education in Israel begins in the yearning of the children to belong to the secret.

Walter Brueggemann

Hearing whispers across the room, we are curious. We want to know what's being said. What are they whispering about? To be included is to be valued. How disappointing to be left on the outside.

One incident is imprinted on my mind. My Boy Scout troop went on a camping trip when I was ten or eleven years old. I must have demanded a lot of attention. I carried a hand puppet on the hike and made a nuisance of myself. Something happened to embarrass me. I was deeply humiliated. The troop arrived at the lodge and went inside to eat and play games. I hid outside in the trees. I remember looking into the brightly lit building at the laughing faces. It was dark and I longed to be inside. My hurt and stubbornness kept me on the outside.

Being left out is particularly painful when we are young. We want to belong. Walter Brueggemann in the quote above is writing about the education of children. It's not just belonging that matters, but belonging to the secret. What is the secret, the key to being part of the culture, the family, the group? We want to know.

Pause for reflection: When do I feel left out? Do I make others feel left out? Do I make an effort to include others who may feel on the outside?

Teaching Moments

But He answered them, "You give them something to eat."

Mark 6:38

The idea of a "teaching moment" comes from Professor Joseph Sittler who I heard speak in Kansas. How many teaching moments occur each day: opportunities to teach a child, a group, another person, or myself?

An old man sat on the Washington State Ferry in a ragged raincoat, picking through a brown paper bag. He pulled out a half-eaten banana. Jesus' words from feeding the five thousand came to me: *"You give them something to eat."* What was I to learn from these words?

At Children's Hospital we waited for Eric to come out of surgery. The snow was deep and Seattle cold. In walked a street person to get warm. He was dirty, unshaven, and dressed in rags. We watched as others moved away in disgust. The man fell asleep and suddenly tumbled onto the floor. Eric's brothers didn't hesitate. They picked the man up and helped him onto a chair. They asked if he was hungry and then drove to McDonalds to buy him a meal.

It was a teaching moment for me. *You give them something to eat.* The message hadn't been lost on Eric's brothers.

Pause for reflection: When have I been surprised by teaching moments? When did I last provide a teaching moment for a child? Who carried a pocket of teaching moments when I was a child?

When Your Sea is in Turmoil

And now the STORM BLAST came, and he was tyrannous and strong: He struck with his o'er taking wings, and chased us south along.

Samuel Taylor Coleridge,
The Rime of the Ancient Mariner

Where do we go when our sea is in turmoil? I sat with a young truck driver in the hospital coffee shop. His twin girls were safe at home. They hadn't been in the truck when it overturned on an icy road. But their mother was in a coma. Until the accident her husband seemed to need nothing except his motorcycle. Things changed quickly. He said to me, "What will I do if she dies?"

The young man's wife and children were regulars at worship. He felt no need for the church. Shortly after his wife recovered, the family came to church. When the service ended he walked down the aisle and enveloped me in a bear hug. "Thank you," he said.

What had I done? Nothing except be there when he needed a friend. I couldn't heal his wife. I had no easy answers to the storm raging in his life. I drank coffee with him and listened. That was enough. When our sea is in turmoil, we need others to see us through the storm.

Pause for reflection: Who has been there to see me through the storms? When have I been there for others? Have difficult times helped me to see others differently?

My Inner Voice

You cannot do kindness too soon, for you never know how soon it will be too late.

Anonymous

How often I've wished I'd followed my instincts and listened to my inner voice. Timetables, obligations, tiredness, and selfishness distract us. At other times I can be just plain lazy.

On call for another pastor I did listen to my inner voice. It was the end of a long week. I was eager to go home. Driving past the home of a man who was very ill, I thought, *I'll stop and* see *him tomorrow. I'm too tired."* What caused me to stop and see him? It proved to be the right thing to do, as he died that night. The next day would have been too late.

I can't take credit for making the right decision. There have been times when I did not listen to my inner voice. That particular incident taught me to listen more carefully. Call it the Holy Spirit, the voice within, or intuition. The voice is there if we're tuned into the lives and people around us.

A Sunday School teacher already late to teach a class saw a man slumped on a bench. Obviously, he was drunk. But the voice in her head told her the man needed help. It turned out she saved his life for he had drifted into a diabetic coma.

Pause for reflection: When have I ignored my inner voice? Did I learn from my deafness? How is my listening today?

49

Personal Gardening

"Emerson quotes Bacon as saying that man is the minister and interpreter of nature. But man has been very slow to see that he is a part of that same Nature of which he is the minister and interpreter."

John Burroughs

I'm not a gardener. But I am from a gardening family. My maternal grandfather hoed two large plots that are part of my childhood memories.

Gail Tsukiyama in *The Samurai's Garden* tells of a Japanese village where leprosy appears among the people. To save their families from shame, the lepers either commit suicide or move from the village to build a separate colony. Matsu, a master gardener, cultivates his own garden in town, but he toils also in the lepers' village. The village is his "personal" garden where he cultivates the lives of those less fortunate. Gail Tsukiyama's novel is a beautiful story of suffering and grace.

The parish ministry has been my personal garden where I share the lives of others. At times the weeds seem to take over. The pastor, counselor, doctor, or care-giver seeks to cultivate grace in this uncertain world.

We all have personal gardens: our families, social group, community, and the larger world. Caring for these others is one way to insure a harvest that benefits everyone.

Pause for reflection: Do I plant the seeds of human kindness? Am I sensitive in dealing with failure? Have I been as eager to celebrate the harvest as I am to pull the weeds?

50

Phoebe's Flowers

You are the light of the world.

Matthew 5:14a

The name Phoebe can be translated as "light." In Greek mythology Phoebe is the moon-goddess. She is also my favorite character in Nathaniel Hawthorne's novel *The House of the Seven Gables.*

The story is about an old couple who live there under the shadow of a curse. They draw the curtains and creep the dark hallways in despair. There is a sense of approaching doom. This changes when Phoebe, a young cousin, comes to live with them. She brings flowers from the garden and light to the dark rooms. As she passes through the house, the old couple begin to live again.

Gloom, despair, meanness and anger easily take over if we let them. How refreshing when someone moves into our lives with laughter. What a change comes over a dark room when light appears.

Some years ago my younger sister died in a automobile accident. My parents sank into despair. They drew the curtains and sat in darkness. They isolated themselves from people and cultivated anger and hopelessness. A few months later another younger sister had a baby and brought him home. The child was our Phoebe, the light that entered my parent's lives. The curtains were opened and the light returned. With this new life, healing began.

Pause for reflection: Do my moods add darkness to the house? In what ways have I been a Phoebe to others? Do I fill my days with darkness or light?

51

Wonder of Wonders

Whether the graced moment, the moment of epiphany, occurs in sitting by a sunset in an open sea or in seeing our newborn baby for the first time, in our first and surest love experience, we learn that the function of grace is not to do, but first to behold.

Matthew Fox

How much more interesting the world would be if we retained the wonder of the child. Why is it so hard for us to behold? The line from the Christmas song comes to me: I wonder as I wander out under the sky. Do I lose the sense of wonder because I do not take time to wander and to see?

Our family vacation took us to the dinosaur museum in Drumheller, Alberta, Canada. Our seven-year-old daughter needed no coaxing to marvel at the fully articulated bones of Tyrannosaurus Rex. As adults we too found it a wonder-full experience. Why should it take something that grand to excite me? Shouldn't I get excited about the first robin of spring, the first star at night, the first snowflake of winter?

Joshua Abraham Heschel was on his deathbed when he said, "Sam, never once in my life did I ask God for success or wisdom or power or fame. I asked for wonder, and he gave it to me."

Pause for reflection: When did I first notice a lack of childhood wonder in myself? Where do I find it easiest to wonder and marvel? How might I increase my ability to wonder?

52

Meandering

It was a sunny day and we walked to town over the old bridge. Our daughter was a toddler. She meandered and stopped to look at every new thing: a rusty nail, a dandelion, a hole in the bridge. Everything was new. Everything was holy.

MEANDERING

Bent at the hips
        as two-year-olds do,
  her nose to the ground
  ruffled bloomers in air
        smelling the dandelion
            nose to yellow eye,

Wanderers never walk straight,
        her curious eye sees,
  sniffs the fence-line rose,
        touches the caterpillar,
        spies a ladybug,
  meanders like a river.

Time is a toddler's world,
        parents wait, patiently
            on the bridge,
  child's eye pressed to the hole
        watching water
            river flow.

Pause for reflection: How much of my life is a straight line? Do I take time to meander and pay attention to what I see? What can I learn from a meandering child?

53

Let the Inner-Child Out

The universe is made of stories, not atoms.

Muriel Ruyeyser

When Ernst Bloch talks about the kingdom of God, he uses the phrase: "shine back into our childhood."

Look into the eyes of a child at play. Notice the spontaneous delight. I smile at their pleasure. Pictures of children who live in poverty, in dysfunctional families, or as victims of war give me pain. Their eyes stare out, hollow and empty. The windows are dark. Shouldn't childhood always be a time of wonder and enjoyment? Adults, too, can lose the light of the inner child.

Our daughter was three years old when we visited a county fair. She saw the giant slide immediately. I'm afraid of heights and tried to divert her attention. She would have none of it and up the ladder we went. I sat her in front of me on a gunnysack. Down we went, certain the ride would scare her. My wife, at the bottom of the slide saw, our daughter's bright eyes grow large as if she were about to cry. Instead a big grin spread across her face and she said, AGAIN! That's how the kingdom of God should be for everyone. That's how life should be.

Pause for reflection: When did I last feel spontaneous joy? When am I best able to let the child out and enjoy the moment? What keeps me from letting my inner child out?

54

Frayed and Nibbled

"I am a frayed and nibbled survivor in a fallen world, and I am getting along. I am aging and eaten and have done my share of eating too."

Annie Dillard

Have you been nibbled on this week? Has someone taken a bite out of you? We all expect a little nibbling from mosquitoes. We are surprised when the bites come from another person. The question is, why does it happen so often?

I've been nibbled on a few times and have been bitten at other times. This is no place to show my own scars. What is the best way to handle nibbles and bites? They are especially painful when they come from close friends we know. They sting with a vengeance.

I've also experienced a great deal of grace. As a young graduate student I was called to the president's office. He was a kind-hearted, gracious man and confided in me that he'd heard of inappropriate behavior on my part. He simply asked me to do the right thing. There was no accusation, anger, or punishment. He did not bite. It was a moment of pure grace. It changed my behavior at the time and my attitude toward others who make poor decisions. Kindness and understanding gets better results than nibbling.

Pause for reflection: When was I last nibbled on? When did I last nibble on someone else? Have I found a way to handle the bites rather than react in anger?

55

Smelling the Roses

It is not death that is the tragedy of life… (but) what you let die when you are alive.

Robert Muller

"*To wake up is to be given back your life again,*" writes Fredrick Buechner. To open our eyes to a new day is like the child seeing a dandelion for the first time. When do we start taking such delights for granted? I remember bouncing out of bed as a child. "What is going to happen today?" In middle age getting up was part of the routine. In old age my body says, stay in bed a little longer.

I remember those great nights of anticipation: the circus train coming to town; a birthday party; Christmas morning; graduation; a wedding day. The naturalist John Burroughs once wrote: *He (man) is forever born anew into the world and experiences new wonder, new joy, new loves, new enthusiasms.*

Most of the time I noticed the roses growing around the house, but, I confess, it was often with a sideways glance as I hurried by. Now that I'm older, I pause more often to smell the roses. The years between childhood and old age can blur the gifts around us. They melt into the background of our schedules and obligations. It seems fitting that they reappear again later in life.

Pause for reflection: What do I notice now that I ignored in earlier years? How might I develop a better sense of seeing? What should I look at more closely today?

Apostles of the Living Light

Slowly, Slowly, they return
to the small woodland let alone:
great trees, outspreading and upright,
apostles of the living light.

Wendell Berry

The young man was thirty-two years old, killed in an avalanche while snowmobiling. I met with his wife, best friend, and parents. They told me how trees were not only his job as a logger, but his recreation. He competed at logger rodeos. His life was much shorter in years than the trees he admired.

I've have had a number of experiences with loggers over the years. Sometimes I've been critical of logging practices and the damage done to the environment. Yet many loggers understand and appreciate the sacredness of a standing forest. Looking up through the forest canopy, the light shines from above and reminds one of a cathedral.

There are sacred moments to be had from these apostles of the living light. One of mine came when I was in college and visited the White Mountains of California. We stood before a stand of Bristlecone Pine, the oldest living trees on the planet. Touching them was to touch the time of Abraham. Why do so many people visit the redwood forests each year? Surely it is to venerate these apostles from the time of Abraham sifting the light from heaven.

Pause for reflection: When was I last still in a sacred forest? Where else do I experience sacred moments? What is it about those moments I remember?

Sacred Places

Ranger Station on main street,
"I'm a traveler,
I want to know the way
to the White Mountains,
& the bristlecone pines"

Gary Snyder

Bristlecone Pines

A hot and dry day
in the White Mountains,
we stand awestruck before
the oldest living trees, their
limbs gnarled like old men
outside a smoke shop.

Bristlecone Pines wear
rings as old as Abraham.
Our young years dwarfed
by four thousand years.

Under glaring sunlight we
tenderly touch the smooth
venerable old souls as we
would a great grandfather
lying in a velvet-lined casket.

Pause for reflection: How do I define the sacred in my life?
Where do I go to be alone with the holy? With whom have I shared sacred moments?

58

Being a Star

...they set out; and there, ahead of them,
went the star...

Matthew 2:9

I'm intrigued by those who follow celebrity magazines. What is it that elevates models, actors, and sports heroes to stardom? The Magi in the Christmas story followed the star. They did not worship it. Yet, we elevate celebrities almost to a position of worship.

So often we overlook those close to us who live heroic lives. In high school Larry was a good athlete and very popular. But it wasn't Larry's athletic records that made people look up to him. It was his kindness.

On his way home from school one afternoon Larry saw a crowd gathered in a field. The shouts grew louder. David, a shy young man, was often the focus of jeers and ridicule. When Larry arrived at the scene he saw David on the ground, covering his face with his hands. Others were cheering as one of the boys kicked David again and again. Without hesitating Larry jumped in and stopped the fight. The crowd dispersed and Larry helped the boy to his feet and walked him home.

I was a young high school student at the time. But the impression Larry made on me that day made him a star to me. He was a star leading the way.

Pause for reflection: Who have been the stars in my life? Why did I look up to them? Have I been a star to someone else?

New Lenses

Jesus said to her, Mary!

John 20:18

You gave me a new name, you called me Dulcinea.

Cervantes, *Don Quixote*

A cartoon shows three pastors in an office flipping a coin. The caption reads: "They are casting lots to see who will go with the middle school kids to camp."

To spend five days at a middle school camp requires an adjustment to one's thinking. Adults have to see eleven to fourteen year olds as they are neither children or adults. It's a matter of putting on different lenses. When this happens middle school kids can be fun.

When Don Quixote sees the harlot, Aldonza, he sees what others do not. She is a waitress by day who serves camel drivers by night. Don Quixote sees beyond this. He calls her, "My Lady."

"Yes, you are my lady," he says, "and I shall give you a new name. I shall call you Dulcinea. You are my Lady, Dulcinea." Don Quixote adjusts his lenses and sees what others cannot see.

When Don Quixote is dying, a broken, despised, and rejected, a Spanish Queen kneels at his bed side. "Who are you?" he asks. She replies, "You gave me a new name, I am your Lady."

What would the world be like if we knew how to adjust our lenses when we look at others?

Pause for reflection: Do I judge others prematurely? When have I been wrong about someone? When have I been judged wrongly myself?

60

To Be Valued

Do we learn to matter to the world? We matter, not because of our achievements but because we are loved by God and loved by the people around us."

Harold S. Kushner

As a high school student I was active in church. Away from church I was a typical teenager, needing to be noticed and valued by others. Being valued is essential to our health.

Because of my activity in the church I often called the pastor's home. Mrs. Storvick, the pastor's wife, an energetic, caring, and sometimes brash personality answered the phone. "Hello, Mrs. Storvick, this is just Gene," I said shyly. At this point there was a long pause. Had she heard me? Then came her booming voice: "You are not just Gene, you are a child of God!" If I needed to be valued I always got my money's worth when I talked to Mrs. Storvick.

Perhaps that's the best way to see one another. We are not just teenagers, just doctors, just mothers or fathers. It isn't that simple. We are special, unique, and should be valued. If people feel undervalued they express negative emotions they do not understand. When I began to see that I was valued by another person my confidence grew and I was able to move forward. Value is a gift we can give one another.

Pause for reflection: What people affirmed me when I was growing up? How have I shown others they are valued? When did I last feel valued?

61

Jazzing Up Jesus

*Faster than a speeding bullet, more powerful
than a locomotive, able to leap tall buildings
in a single bound. It's Superman! Strange visitor
from another planet who came to earth . . .*

We're all familiar with the Adventures of Superman from comic books, newspapers, and film. We like a character who can overcome obstacles and keep us safe from harm. Robert Capon, a writer-theologian, writes: *Almost nobody resists the temptation to jazz up the humanity of Christ.*

I struggle not to make more of Jesus than Jesus made of himself. In spite of the work of scholars and attempts to discover the historical Jesus, we're left with little information about Jesus. The early gospels represent each writer's perception of who Jesus was at that time.

This leaves us with a crossword puzzle, so many lines down and so many across. How do we fill in the blanks? Robert Capon is right. We can't help but jazz up Jesus. It is a danger in preaching, teaching, and daily life. Unconsciously we do think of Jesus as arriving from another planet willing to do anything we ask. Yet it's difficult to identify with Superman. It's the thick-rimmed glasses-wearing Clark Kent we understand. I find myself becoming more comfortable with the Jesus who weeps than the one who leaps tall buildings with a single bound.

Pause for reflection: Should Jesus be elevated to a position of worship? What speaks most to me, Jesus' humanity or divinity? What characteristics of Jesus appeal to me?

Living in a Briar Patch

"Born and bred n' a Briar patch, Brier Fox," says he,
"born and bred in a briar patch."

Uncle Remus

In the cotton fields the slaves sang, *This world is not my home, I'm just a passing through.* Perhaps it was of comfort to know that the present drudgery and servitude would not last forever. There was a better place.

But Brier Rabbit had it right. This world is our home, prickly cactus and all. I find comfort listening to elderly people who, have been through the wars. They've found ways to survive and find peace of mind. I remind myself that the promised land usually comes after a sojourn in the desert.

I sat in a pre-marriage session with an elderly couple. The groom, in his sixties, was obviously uncomfortable. I mentioned this and he said, "I know you have a lot of education, but you're young. I doubt you have much to say that's going to make a difference." The man had worked all his life with his hands. Book-learning didn't impress him. Then I showed him my calloused hands from working in a trade. I had immediate credibility. We're all born and bred in the briar patch. Credibility comes from acknowledging that we share the same experiences.

Pause for reflection: When did I first discover that daily life was not always easy? Have I learned to accept hardship and failure? What coping mechanisms do I use in times of struggle?

63

Entrances and Exits

The rabbit-hole went straight on like a tunnel for some way, and then dipped suddenly down, . . .

Alice's Adventures in Wonderland

Children's stories remind us how easy it is to escape into a magical world: through the wardrobe, down the rabbit hole, caught up in a tornado, by the gate into the secret garden. The places we entered as children were magical.

"Come, cross into a new life," Jesus invites the fishermen on the Sea of Galilee. "I will make you fishers of men." It must have sounded magical to those who worked every day trying to get a living from the sea. Was it an invitation to something new, an escape into new adventures? We're told they left their nets to follow this stranger.

What seems an entrance is often an exit from something else. There was a certain amount of risk for those first disciples. We've all experienced times of venturing forth into something new and leaving behind what is familiar and comfortable.

I've experienced this kind of entrance-exit each time I've left one congregation to serve another. There was great expectation as I moved to another community. There was great sadness as I left an old and comfortable group of friends. Our lives are a series of entrances and exits?

Pause for reflection: What is my fondest memory of a joyful entrance? What has been my most painful experience of leaving? What memories of childhood do I have of entering a magical place?

Deep Listening

Hear, O heavens, and listen, O earth, . . .

Isaiah 1:2

I've spent much of my life listening to others. Conversations have taken place in my office, in nursing homes, hospitals, prisons, and family homes. Parish ministry is often about visiting people casually or in times of crisis. Have I listened deeply? I know there are times when I did. There were other times when I was in too much of a hurry or impatient. Listening to another person is a gift that must be practiced and refined over time.

I am attracted to authors who honed their listening skills, writers like Henry David Thoreau, John Burroughs, Loren Eiseley, Chet Raymo, Annie Dillard, and Anne Morrow Lindberg. These men and women were *deep listeners*. Much of their listening was to the natural world. They listened to the change of seasons, the flight of birds, the silent speech of flowers. Each in their own way tuned in to the rhythms of life.

I wonder if deep listening will become a lost art with the constant use of cell phones. Will our eyes focused on cell phone screens disconnect us from face to face encounters? Isaiah invites the very universe to listen, It's an invitation to listen deeply; not with selective hearing, but quietly with expectation and respect.

Pause for reflection: Who have been the good listeners in my life? How might improve my listening skills today? When did I last listen intently to someone?

65

Mending Humpty Dumpty

Humpty Dumpty sat on a wall.
Humpty Dumpty had a great fall.

All the king's horses,
and all the king's men,
couldn't put Humpty together again.

Children's Nursery Rhyme

Mathew Fox writes: "Myths contain wisdom and a trip into our mythological childhood may well make us wiser concerning the meaning and practice of compassion."

No one goes through life without falling off the wall. We break into pieces and wonder if anyone will come to our rescue. At four o'clock on a Sunday afternoon I walked into a police station to see the fallen faces of a sixteen year-old's parents. The fragments were unmistakable. Their lives were shattered and there was no one to put them back together again.

We see the gift of healing in Jesus, Buddha, Gandhi, Mother Teresa, and countless others. But is it our vocation as well? We are all called to recognize the broken and bring compassion to cracked lives.

To me as a child Humpty Dumpty appeared comical, his big head lying on the ground. As adults the story takes on new meaning. We know that we are Humpty Dumpty. We hope someone will come to our rescue when needed. When others fall we are called to be all the king's men and women who come to pick up the pieces and heal the hurt.

Pause for reflection: Who has come to my rescue? When was the last time I encountered another person's brokenness? How have times of crisis changed me?

A Circle of Quiet

My special place is a small brook in a green glade,
a circle of quiet from which there is no visible sign of
human beings.

Madeline L'Engle

What strikes me about Jesus the busy pastor is not the number of people that needed him, but the calm in which he met their needs. When there were too many people to feed, a Roman officer's daughter to attend to, or squabbling disciples to deal with; Jesus didn't get rattled.

In several places we're told Jesus went in the morning to a lonely place alone to listen for the Koi Yahweh, the voice of God. Jesus knew how to deal with day to day pressures.

I'm not as disciplined with time-out as self-care. When I have taken time to rest I've been amazed at how much more effective I am in accomplishing necessary tasks. When a sixteen- year-old boy was killed in a shooting accident, I needed a quiet place to gather my thoughts. A family in the parish offered me their back porch when I needed to be alone. On that occasion my circle of quiet overlooked an aspen grove and became the place where I could listen for the Koi Yahweh, the voice of God.

Pause for reflection: Where is my circle of quiet today? Do I have a regular time when I empty myself of worries and obligations? What keeps me from taking time out for myself?

Circle of Quiet II

The profane never hear music, the holy ever hear it.

Henry David Thoreau:
Journal Entry for June 28, 1840

The Aspen Grove

A young boy died I knew well
in the fall of a certain year.
I went alone to the aspen grove,
leave falling, paper tears.

Surrounded by aspen breath,
forest voices prayed,
let grief fall in autumn
healing is on the way.

Comfort came as whispers,
wind-born through aspen limbs,
softly as a cathedral choir,
singing of grief within.

"Do not move," my body said,
"Listen to these dying things.
Remember him, whom you loved,
these trees will bloom again."

Pause for reflection: What kind of music do find most healing? In what way does nature speak to me? In what circumstances do I need to find a place to be alone?

Hidden Teachers

If you do not expect it, you will not find the unexpected,
for it is hard to find and difficult.

Hereclitus

Most lessons are learned outside the classroom from parents, grand-parents, pastors, coaches, and friends. At other times we are taught by silent and hidden teachers.

Some teachers are children or strangers we pass in the shopping mall. Much of my learning comes from quiet conversations with authors in a good book. We learn in hidden ways from hidden teachers.

The ancient Greeks were familiar with hidden teachers. They spoke of the Logos: wisdom, word. Logos was a seed carried by the wind. It took on a life of its own and moved among people, revealing truth at just the right moment.

Hidden teachers come to us in stories and parables. They are found in in conversation with a farmer in a coffee shop and with the elderly in a nursing home.

The poet Gerard Manley Hopkins dreaded the coming of winter. He didn't notice the glory of fall. Suddenly he began to focus on the beauty of the harvest he hadn't seen before and he wrote:

> These things,
> These things were here and but the beholder
> Wanting.

Teachers are all around us if only we take time to look and listen.

Pause for reflection: How difficult do I find it to listen quietly? When was the last time I was surprised by something new? From what unexpected person did I learn something?

69

Idleness

To assure the greatest efficiency in the dart, the harpooners of this world must start to their feet from out of idleness, and not from out of toil.

Herman Melville, *Moby Dick*

I need a hiding place, a place where there is quiet for renewal. There I can slow down my body and mind. A hiding place might be found in the forest, a room, or in a garden. It needs to be a place where escape from the turmoil and obligations of the day is possible.

If I'm always giving, my energy runs low. It becomes necessary to restock in order to have something to bring back into the community. Without solitude I have nothing to give to others. Without community what I gain in solitude is lost. Madeleine L'Engle wrote about her *Circle of Quiet* where she would go over a stone bridge to a brook where she could be alone.

The place doesn't matter, but the opportunity to replenish is important. I like the scene painted by Herman Melville in *Moby Dick*. All the oarsmen are busy pulling and straining to reach their quarry. Only one person in the boat is idle, the harpooner. Why does he sit still, harpoon ready? Because he must be prepared for what happens next. It is out of idleness that his best work is done.

Pause for reflection: Where is my circle of quiet? When did I last replenish myself? When do I need such a place the most?

Living in a Bubble

Jesus hung out with ragamuffins.

Brenan Manning

It occurred to me that I live in a bubble when I visited a Hispanic group and listened to them talk about their struggles. I thought I understood how they felt; then someone said, "You can't understand until you have lived our lives."

Invited to attend a Compassionate Friends meeting of parents who had lost children in death, I experienced my bubble. I'd worked with grieving families and thought I knew how they felt. The abrupt answer I received was, "You cannot know unless you have lost a child."

At first I was hurt by these responses. With more thought I knew they were right. I was not Hispanic. I had not lived as a minority. I had not lost a child. I could sympathize and try to understand, but it was not the same as being in those situations..

The story of the child born without an immune system brings tears to my eyes. He lived in a sterile bubble for nine years without being touched by his parents except through specially designed gloves. When old enough he decided to leave the bubble and ran to be held by his mother.

I'm thankful I've not experienced such isolation. Yet I do live in my own bubble. I hope it doesn't prevent me from trying to understand another person.

Pause for reflection: When do I feel most alone? What keeps me separate from other people? How do I feel when I am shut out?

Simple Words. Simple Actions

The theory of a thing is so much easier than the practice!

John Burroughs, *Riverby*

I haven't shaken hands with a president. Ken Griffey Jr. hasn't called me on the phone. In truth neither of those things would make a difference. What has made a difference to me are the small actions of people.

On my fiftieth birthday the congregation I was serving bought me a new wardrobe. Were they ashamed of the way I dressed? No, it was their way of thanking me. That simple action has stayed with me all these years.

The story is told about Pinkus Zuckerman, the violin virtuoso teaching at a summer music camp. On the last day each student played before the master. At the end of each performance Zukerman picked up his own violin and played the note he thought might be improved. The last student preformed and there was quiet in the auditorium. The master went and picked up his instrument. He lifted the violin to his chin, lowered it and placed it back in its case without playing a note. What a unforgettable message that simple action carried to the student. A simple action never to be forgotten.

Pause for reflection: When did someone speak a simple word to me that made a difference? What simple action do I remember? When have I said something or done something that made a difference to someone?

Room to Fly

*Can you cleanse your inner vision until you see
nothing but the light?*

Tao Te Ching 10

I find the invitation to be still a difficult one. Blaise Pascal once suggested that the world's trouble is due to the fact that we cannot sit still in a room. We must chatter, gamble, or hunt for something. I'm with Pascal. It is hard to sit still. And yet I know it is in stillness and quiet that space is cleared for personal growth.

One of my favorite stories is about the wealthy man who hired a Japanese artist to paint a mural on his living room wall. The man gave the artist keys to his home to paint while he was on vacation. When the client returned he stared at the wall. He'd paid for a mural and what he saw was a small drawing in one corner of a bird in a tree.

"Where is the mural?" asked the client. "You have painted a tree and a small bird. Why have you left the rest of the wall blank?"

"The bird must have room to fly," answered the artist.

If I am to fly I must give myself space for reflection in order to spread my wings.

Pause for reflection: What keeps me from taking time out for myself? What does my need to be busy say about my character? What do I gain and what do I lose by being busy?

73

Gift Givers

*Like the Semitic nomads, we live in a desert with many
lonely travelers who are looking for a moment of peace,
for a fresh drink and for a sign of encouragement . . .*

Henri Nouwen, *The Wounded Healer*

I'm attracted to cultures who provide hospitality to strangers seemingly
without question. It seems strange to Americans who are suspicious and
often afraid of those who come to our doors.

The practice of hospitality is suggested by Jesus in sending out disciples.
They were to take nothing with them, but expect a welcome when they
came to a house.

Hospitality is built into the Native American culture. Strangers are never
refused. There is a strong sense of caring for the other as seen in the practice of the "giveaway." During a special occasion, a wedding or a death in
a family, the host family spreads out a blanket on which gifts are placed.
Everyone in the village is invited to take a gift.

I experienced this hospitality on a visit with kids to the Nez Perce res-
ervation in Lapwai, Idaho. During the Powwow visitors were invited to
dance the circle dance. The tribal members formed the inner circle and
visitors formed the outer circle. As the circles moved in opposite direc-
tions we shook hands with the dancers, receiving a warm welcome.

Pause for reflection: When have I felt most welcomed by another person? When have I felt least welcomed? How might I present a
more welcoming presence?

Stepping Away

Thou, O God, art as a hiding place from the wind, and a covert from the storm, as rivers of water in a dry place, as the shadow of a great rock in a weary land.

Isaiah 32:2

It is always a short step to peace of mind. Henry David Thoreau

Stepping Away

I wish I had known
the art of stepping away,
visiting a shaman's place,
to sit in a cool cave,
peering out into daylight
over valleys below, where
frenzy beats a rhythmic pace,
chaos makes room for fear,
anger follows like a friend.

We become emotional debris
swept daily into dust bins,
scraps of life without peace.

Old age brings time to see
from a cave's opening
into the valleys below,
hear voices dent the sky.
Perhaps it's not too late
when turmoil knocks
to teach our children
when to step away
to find peace of mind.

Pause for reflection: Have I found ways to deal with a frantic world? Have I been a calming presence to others? Where is the place I go to find peace of mind?

75

Why Do Bugs Land On Hats?

*When you wake in the morning, called by God to be
a self again, if you want to know who you are, watch
your feet. Because where your feet take you, that is who
you are.*

Fredrick Buechner

Children play with abandon. They enjoy the moment. Small children do not stop to ask, "Who am I?" In early childhood life is enough.

Our family traveled to Dinosaur Provincial Park in Alberta, Canada to see where paleontologists were digging. We touched the bones of triceratops with one finger. That was exciting, but it was the question from a child just before our hike that I remember most.

Our daughter and another young boy waited anxiously for the hike to begin. The Ranger asked if there were any questions, expecting to be asked about dinosaurs. The small boy raised his hand. "Yes, young man," said the Ranger.

"Why do bugs land on hats?" asked the boy. The Rangers had no idea how to answer the boy's question.

Children live in the moment. The questions they ask are of the moment. There will be time enough later in life to question and ponder larger questions. Perhaps like the child on the dinosaur walk it is enough to watch where my feet take me.

Pause for reflection: When did I last experience pure joy? How much time do I spend over the big questions? Do I waste time worrying about things I cannot control?

Have Salt in Yourselves

Armenians, I read, salt their newborn babies.

Annie Dillard

I can usually tell if a person is distressed, angry, excited, or just plain bored. But when I meet someone who has lost the will to live, I ask, when did they lose their saltiness?

In her book *Holy the Firm* Annie Dillard explains how the Jews and Armenians in the time of the prophets washed a baby in water, salted him, and wrapped him in clothes. Salt became a life-giving property binding the child to the covenant. . . . *it is a covenant of salt forever.* Jesus calls his followers *the salt of the earth.*

What happens if we lose our taste for life? I visited an elderly man in a nursing home who was once a vibrant human being, working on his farm and raising a family. Now he was broken, sleeping most of the time in a dark room. The only time I saw him smile was when my wife brought our newborn daughter to show him. For a moment there was a twinkle in his eye.

Salt is good, says Jesus. *But if the salt has lost its saltiness, how will you season it?* Will I lose my saltiness? If that should happen I hope someone will be there to pass the salt.

Pause for reflection: Do I know someone today who has lost their saltiness? Who do I know that conveys a zest for life? What can I do to retain my saltiness?

The House of Lost Parents

Unless you call out, who will open the door?

Ethiopian Proverb

When a very small child is lost, panic sets in. On Disneyland's Main Street, people were crowded heel to toe. I turned and stumbled into a small child who was in tears. I picked him up so he wouldn't be trampled by the herd. What to do?

A Disney worker directed me to the House of Lost Parents. Of course, I thought, Disneyland is a child's world. It's not children who get lost, but parents. I found the small house where other children waited to be rescued. Their parents had obviously gotten lost.

Where is the House of Lost Souls? I'm not thinking of souls in terms of salvation. Where can I go when I've lost my way? Where is the place I can go where I will be welcomed? It might be a real door or simply a door in the heart of someone who stumbles over me at a difficult time. Most of us will stop at the cry of a small child. How many of us stop when an adult is lost and needs our help?

Can I be that house, paying attention, listening to the words and feelings around me, ready to open the door for another person?

Pause for reflection: When was the last time I really felt lost? How did I find my way again? When was I last able to listen to the cry of a lost soul and provide help?

The Whistler

When I was a boy I learned after many
discouragements to play on a tin whistle.

David Grayson, *The Friendly Road*

Writer David Grayson recalls an old man who sat on the shady side of an old hotel playing a tin whistle. It so affected Grayson that he bought a tin whistle and learned to play.

Ancient shamans and spiritual leaders were whistlers, attracting people by their playing. The music wasn't always melodious, as witnessed by the prophets. Jesus, Buddha, and Mohammed piped their tunes to call people to a better life.

I'll never forget my fifth grade teacher who at a certain period after lunch invited us to lay our heads on our desks and close our eyes. As we relaxed, she walked between aisles and whistled. She was a professional whistler and her talent was much different than the sound you hear on the street. Her music was soothing and comforting.

We have the opportunities to do what this teacher did. We may not whistle or sing, but the opportunities are there to bring comfort and peace to others. I can walk down the aisles of a market, or a hallways in my home and become a calming presence to another person.

Pause for reflection: Who do I known whose peaceful presence fills the room? Have I been able to provide peace of mind when it was needed? How might I practice the art of bringing comforting music to others?

Drowned Cake

Living the spiritual life is the attitude you hold in your mind when you are down on your knees scrubbing the steps

Evelyn Underhill

The woman was excited about her husband coming from the hospital with a clean bill of health. Two blocks from the hospital, he died of a massive coronary.

How do we handle events that rip us apart? It is, of course, easy to give simple answers. Rabbi Kushner told an audience about the many responses people gave after the death of his nine year- old son from progeria, the aging disease. Someone said, "Aren't you glad you have another son?" It was said in kindness without thinking. How could one son take the place of another?

How do I cope when the expected celebration is cut short? I do not recommend easy answers. On most occasions a comforting presence is more important than any words offered. Ultimately it's a person's attitude towards life that makes the difference. If I see myself as a victim I will find it difficult to cope with disappointment. If I understand that rain falls on the just and on the unjust, I will find a way to move ahead and bake another cake.

Pause for reflection: Are there times when I've felt victimized? How do I move on from *why me?* Have the crises in my life made me a stronger person?

80

Faith Leaping

I love the recklessness of faith. First you leap,
and then you grow wings.

William Sloan Coffin

Soren Kierkegaard talks about a leap of faith in which, in spite of all odds, a person says, "I believe nevertheless." The best example I know of this leap of faith is related by Henry Nouwen when he tells of a great trapeze troop.

Nouwen asked the leader of the troop how they were able to do what they did. The leader explained: "You have a flyer and you have a catcher. The catcher, catches. The flyer, flies."

How simple it sounds. The trick, of course, is that the flyer must have complete trust in the catcher in order to let go of the trapeze.

Faith is letting go and leaping into the presence of that which we cannot see. We trust there is another there to catch us. We live with the fear that there is no net. Faith is flying through the air, trusting that the catcher will catch us.

Jesus suggests in Luke's Gospel that when we try to make ourselves secure, we lose. It's in the insecurity of our lives that we learn to trust. From a religious perspective faith means letting go of false securities and falling into the hands of the divine presence.

Pause for reflection: When have I felt most vulnerable? Am I a person who needs all the answers before making a decision? Has my ability to trust grown weaker or stronger?

No Good, Very Bad News

I went to sleep with gum in my mouth and now there's gum in my hair . . . I think I'll move to Australia.

Alexander's No Good Very Bad Day

When I read a violent Bible passage on Sunday morning my lips speak the words, but my mind shouts: "Where is the Good News?"

Was the writer having a bad day? If so, my advice is, "Don't write on those days. Your doom and gloom is not good news." Perhaps the purpose in these difficult passages is to point us in a new direction: there is a better way. Amos, the prophet wrote:

> Take away from me the noise of your songs;
> I will not listen to the melody of your harps,
> but let justice roll down like waters,
> and righteousness, like an ever-flowing stream.

Amos points me in a new direction. Do not blister my skin with threats and abuse. I don't want to hear the noise of your songs. If the melody of your harps put me to sleep, I will have none of them. The good news calls me to a better way, to justice and better days. Like Alexander in the children's book, I do not have to go to Australia to find a better way.

Pause for reflection: On a bad day do I find myself a pessimist or optimist? When bombarded with bad news, do I tune in or tune out? What kind of news do I bring to others?

Being Myself and Loving It!

"Real isn't how you are made," said the Skin Horse.
"It's a thing that happens to you."

The Velveteen Rabbit

I've been self-conscious most of my life. As a young teenager I insisted on wearing long-sleeved shirts to school. I didn't want others to know I was growing hair on my arms. This vanity, of course, follows us through life. Later in life we lose our hair, acquire wrinkles, age spots, and excess weight. And so there is Botox, diet plans, personal trainers, and complexion remedies.

I admire those who accept themselves and understand that life is a process and we cannot return to our youth or deny our age.

I like the words of the Skin Horse. "Real isn't how you are made. It's a thing that happens to you." And we find that out if our lives are spent with others who love us we become real.

A teacher once said something to me that changed my thinking. She took me aside after class and said, "In this class you seem to be the most at home in your own skin." That comment surprised me and affirmed me. That, of course, is what being a self is all about, to be who we are at that particular time in our life.

Pause for reflection: What bothers me most about myself? Is there anything that keeps me from being myself? Am I still trying to prove myself to others?

83

Giving Back

*For a human character to reveal truly exceptional
qualities, one must have the good fortune to be able to
observe its performance over many years.*

Jean Giono, *The Man Who Planted Trees*

In 1913 Jean Giono went on a walking tour in Provence. He met shepherd who was planting oaks, beeches, and birches. The land was dry and wasted. By planting trees water was preserved, dry streambeds filled and seeds germinated over the land. When Giono returned to Provence after two world wars he found villages and farms where once a desert had stood.

Giono's story is a great example of giving back what we have received. In forty years of ministry I have given my time, energy, and myself to others. It's a good thing to know that my efforts were worthwhile. But I have received much more. Many have been generous in giving gifts, time, and themselves to me and my family. We have planted trees in each other's gardens and they have flourished.

I'm often surprised by the generosity of people. In a world where the code phrase seems to be "get yours while you can," I've found generous, giving people. On many occasions I have received a quiet and sincere embrace from a grieving family even when much had been lost.

Pause for reflection: When did I last give back to someone out of genuine thankfulness? When did I last write a thank-you note? How might I give back this week?

The Tin Box

*To be looking elsewhere for miracles is to me a sure sign
of ignorance that everything is miraculous.*

Abraham Maslow

Children are wonderfully awake. They seldom tire of what's new and interesting. They marvel at the world around them.

On Thanksgiving Day my two-year-old niece visited with her family. Not interested in the turkey her eyes spotted the treasures in our home. While the rest of us ate Abby searched the house, examining everything within reach. She carried a tin box and stuffed it with colorful things. First a checker piece, then a chess piece. She found a bowl of shells. She came to a tea cup, but did not touch it. I peeked around the door and heard her say, "Isn't that beautiful."

No one asked Abby to pay attention to these things. All was interesting and spoke to her. What an interesting world it is when one is a child. Observing and absorbing is what a child does. Marveling and delighting is in the child's nature. Wandering and meandering is how a child gets about.

I still enjoy learning. I don't delight in the same way as I did, but I am beginning to wander and meander. Everything is miraculous to a child. Perhaps this is what Jesus meant when he said, "To such belong the kingdom of God."

Pause for reflection: When did I last truly delight in something? When did I last find myself meandering? What is in my collector's box?

The Song We Hear Is the Song We Sing

*The ancients sang their way all over the world. They
sang the rivers and ranges, salt-pans and sand dunes.
They hunted, ate, made love, danced, killed: wherever
their tracks led they left a trail of music.*

Bruce Chatwin, *The Songlines*

Music seems to be natural to humans. Playing and singing songs is
something we hold in common and is reflected in songs, mantra, and
liturgy.

I'm most familiar with the Christian forms of worship. Of course the music in worship didn't begin with Christianity. The four canticles in Luke's
Gospel began long before the established church. These songs in the early
chapters are familiar to us as: The Gloria in Excelsis; The Magnificat; The
Benedictus; and The Nunc Dimittis.

Songs are more than entertainment as witnessed by the Aboriginals of
Australia. Bruce Chatwin tells of the Aboriginal totem ancestors, who are
thought to have scattered a trail of words and music along the paths they
traveled. Their dream-tracks lay over the land like footprints. He writes:
"If you knew the song of your ancestor, you could always find your way
across country."

The deeper songs we sing are the songs we heard while growing up. These
songs come from our culture, our family traditions, and the experiences
that have shaped us.

Pause for reflection: What dream-tracks did my ancestors leave
for me to follow? What words and melodies did I learn that reflect who
I am today? What musical notes have I left behind?

Singers of Life

They sang under the brooding shadow of the raven.
In simple truth they had forgotten the raven, for they
were the singers of life, and not of death.

Loren Eiseley, *The Judgment of the Birds*

Ravens and crows have represented the dark, threatening side of life in literature and song. In *An Exaltation of Larks* James Lipton we find "A Murder of Crows." In Loren Eiseley's essay, he witnesses firsthand the murderous intent of the raven as it devours a nestling. Eiseley simply points out a natural part of life. He goes on to show us that life cannot stop there.

Life must go on even after the most devastation. In Eiseley's experience on one occasion he witnessed the death of a baby bird, then out of the silence birds began to sing. Even after the frantic objection of the nestling's parents, life went on. Out of grief's silence life, reasserts itself.

How many times have I seen this happen in tragic circumstances? In the days and weeks of suffering, life seems to end. Those who grieve wish they could crawl away and die. But somehow change happens and a word, a song, is heard however tentatively. In that moment we become singers of life and not of death.

Pause for reflection: In what dark moment have I heard these life-giving notes? When and how do I bring healing in a sensitive way? When have I found it most difficult to be a singer of life?

Not to Have, But to Be

There is a realm of time where the goal is not to have but to be, not to own but to give, not to control but to share, not to subdue but to be in accord.

Abraham Joshua Heschel

I admire those in history who are comfortable with standing quietly alone. Few people I know possess the talent for simply being in the moment. We are suspicious of idleness.

If we enter a dentist's waiting room and find it empty, we wonder if he is really a good dentist. Productivity is the measure of one's worth in American society. Should my goal be to work harder so I can have more? Do I need to be in control and subdue all things to my advantage? Where is the time to breathe and be?

I'm a fan of men and women like Henry David Thoreau, John Burroughs, John Muir, Annie Dillard; who find time to observe and live in the world. Again I turn to someone like Loren Eiseley who thought nothing of kneeling in the dessert with a coyote pup and entering a moment in which he could simply be. It was a moment when thoughts of having wre set aside, a time of playfulness.

Pause for reflection: When was the last full day I did nothing productive but enjoy myself? What have I produced in my lifetime that is lasting? Who do I know that is at home with simply being present?

The Gift of Unknown Things

> *I know it was alive and I believe it was conscious.*
> *During the time it was there beneath the boat, I felt a*
> *presence, the kind of certainty of life nearby that you*
> *have when you wake in a dark room and know beyond*
> *doubt that someone else is there with you."*

Lyall Watson

The above description of luminescence reminds me of the Mount of Transfiguration. Lyall Watson encountered a fluorescent cloud that followed his boat. The disciples fell on their knees before a brilliant light. Both events must have been startling.

Experiences of unknown things can be very real and frightening. The disciples tried to describe their experience to others and explained the brilliant light as the glory of God.

As I lay in bed one dark night I was overwhelmed with a feeling that someone was in the room. The feeling became so strong I got out of bed and turned on the bathroom light. The feeling was real, but I cannot explain it.

Luminaries and mysterious feelings in the dark cannot always be explained by theology or science. They suggest to me that I cannot know everything. It's okay to be left with mystery and questions, as the disciples must have been returning from the mountain.

Pause for reflection: What have I experienced that remains a mystery? Am I comfortable with unexplained experiences? Do I read the Transfiguration as a literal event or as an attempt to explain unknown things?

89

To Be a Blessing

Blessing is an attitude toward all of life . . .

Madeleine L'Engle

Ancient peoples lived with blessings and curses. Living close to nature they saw natural disasters as curses, and rain over dry lands as blessings. We haven't moved far away from this easy explanation. Newscasters still talk of hurricanes and tornadoes as "acts of god."

Someone said to me, "we are blessed to live in such a beautiful place." I didn't disagree. But it's an easy comment to a complex idea. If one is blessed, there must be someone behind the blessing. It's assumed by most people that someone is God or another deity. That was the under-standing of the writers of the bible. *Blessed are the poor in spirit for to them belong the kingdom of heaven.* The writer understood that there is one who blesses the poor.

What does it mean to be a blessing? Do I initiate a blessing or is there another who blesses through me? To bless simply means to bring happiness, good will, and prosperity to another person.

Each of us has opportunities every day to be a blessing to others. As Madeleine L'Engle suggests, to be a blessing is an attitude toward life lived out on a daily basis.

Pause for reflection: When was I last a blessing to someone? When was I last blessed? How might I be a blessing to my family and my friends?

Walking the Woods

More things are learnt in the wood than from books;
trees and rocks will teach you things not to be heard
elsewhere.

St. Bernard of Clairvaux

There's a great difference between knowledge and wisdom. In our day information can be acquired by clicking a button on a keyboard. What will the weather be like tomorrow? Who was Ingrid Bergman? Where is the Mona Lisa? Acquiring facts is easier today than ever before. But will a person retain this information and be able to use it?

In my younger days after graduate school I began work in a congregation of people who had life experience. "You have book knowledge," said one man. "But do you know anything about life?" Higher education did not give me the credibility I needed.

"Walking the woods" is another way of saying wisdom is acquired by living. How I apply what I know comes from living and learning skills that will help in unforeseen circumstances. To walk in the woods with someone who knows the woods from observation over many years is different than listening to someone who knows them only from books.

The four traits of a Sioux warrior were bravery, fortitude, generosity, and wisdom. Wisdom was the hardest to attain and was usually a gift of age. Perhaps this is what St. Bernard discovered.

Pause for reflection: Looking back on my youth, how have I changed? Have I become wiser rather than more knowledgeable? Am I happy with where I am today?

Holiness in Time

The holiness of the chosen day is not something at which to stare and from which we must humbly stay away. It is holy not away from us. It is holy unto us.

Abraham Joshua Heschel, *The Sabbath*

Alice falls down the rabbit hole. Children fall into fantasy worlds. I fall into dreams. We leave the present for another time and another place. Perhaps these escapes save us from ourselves.

Loren Eiseley writes: "As adults, we are preoccupied with living. As a consequence, we see little. At the approach of age some men look about them at last and discover the hole in the hedge leading to the unforeseen. By then, there is frequently no child companion to lead them safely through."

How many holy places have I passed? How many holes in the hedge did I wonder about?

Were there days when a yellow-brick road lay before me and I chose another path? The cornfields of Iowa was such a place, swaying high over head they were magic places to hide and scary places where one could get lost.

In later life time alone or a new book bring me close the new hedge. Perhaps a "second" childhood meant to give us back the dreams and imagination of childhood. Don't forget the holy places in time. They are still there.

Pause for reflection: What magical moments do I remember from my childhood? What delights me most now? Do I still look for holy places in time?

Friendly Spaces

Lawd, everything nailed down is comin' loose. . .

Roark Bradfore, *Green Pastures*

In downtown Vancouver, B.C., stands Christ Cathedral. I became acquainted with this Anglican Church during two years of Spiritual Direction. As I entered the spiritual director's room I was drawn instantly into a place of quiet. Everything slowed down and for an hour it was as if I had entered a different time zone.

Henri Nouwen describes such a place in these words: *Healing is the humble, but also very demanding task of creating and offering friendly empty space where strangers can reflect on their pain and suffering without fear, and find the confidence that makes them look for new ways right in the center of their confusion."*

I know of no better description of spiritual direction or of our need to find a gifted listener.

Perhaps this was what attracted people to Jesus and others like the Dalai Lama. Such people exude a quiet presence, an invitation to come sit for awhile.

Can I become such a room for someone who needs a healing presence? The key, of course, is to be at peace within oneself. To be that room is to be an open door a person can look through and see not turmoil, but calm. How do I create such a friendly space?

Pause for reflection: How many times have I tried to muddle through on my own? Who do I know who has the skill of deep listening? Do I know of a quiet healing place?

Halos Too Tight

*No man is an island entire of itself; every man is a
piece of the continent, a part of the maine,...*

John Donne

Brenan Manning tells the story of a man who complained to his doctor about a terrible headache. "Do you smoke, drink, or carouse at night?" asked the doctor. With the examination over the doctor realized his patient is a little too self-righteous. "Is the pain in your head a sharp, shooting pain?"

"That's it," said the man.

The doctor responded, "Simple, my dear fellow! The trouble is you have your halo on too tight. All you need is to loosen it a bit."

It's a funny story and true of many of us who belong to benevolent organizations. It doesn't matter if it's a church, synagogue, or a service organization. Too often we represent people unable to loosen up.

I remember a conversation with a man who didn't come to worship because he had only overalls to wear. "I don't feel comfortable with all those shirts and ties. I know people will look down on me if I come."

How uncomfortable I make people when my halo is too tight. How much damage I do when I exclude others because they are different. Perhaps a sign on the mirror in the morning will help: CHECK YOUR HALO!

Pause for reflection: Have I ever felt excluded? Have I been guilty of making a quick judgment about someone? Am I more tolerant now than when I was younger?

Loneliness

Across the sky, the clouds move
Across the fields, the wind,
Across the fields the lost child
Of my mother wanders.

Hermann Hesse

I'm reminded of Jesus' words: *Foxes have holes, and birds of the air have nests; but the Son of Man has nowhere to lay his head.* Who hasn't felt lonely? Loneliness is different from being alone. Is loneliness wishing for something I cannot have? Is it a longing I cannot get beyond?

The best I can do to explain loneliness is describe a time when I felt lonely. It was after a long trip by bus from Minnesota to California. I was a young adult running away. Loneliness often comes when we are running away. I had no place to go. I knew no one in Los Angeles when I arrived. I felt lonely as I watched others who seemed to have a purpose.

I finally called the one family I knew that lived forty miles away. They invited me to their home. It was a gracious act. Staying with the family did not remove the loneliness, but it helped me move through it to a better time.

In reading the words of Hermann Hesse and Jesus I'm aware that everyone experiences loneliness. From experience I know the other side of loneliness is welcome. Beyond welcome is a return to normality.

Pause for reflection: When have I felt most lonely? Have I recognized loneliness in others? How have I learned to climb out of loneliness?

Not Ugly Ducklings, But Swans

*I never dreamed of so much happiness
when I was the ugly duckling.*

Hans Christian Andersen, *The Ugly Duckling*

It's my favorite story. For Hans Christian Anderson it was autobiographical. Yet in spite of his poor self image it is his statue that stands in the most public place in Copenhagen.

We dream of what we might be if we didn't think of ourselves as unwanted. Ugliness can be a perception laid upon us by others or a feeling that comes from within us. Like the Ugly Duckling we feel born out of place in a duck yard. We see ourselves as unwanted. It isn't long before we begin to accept that we are on the outside.

"Can you lay eggs?" asked the mother duck. It's an accusation. Can you prove your worthiness? Will you ever amount to anything? Anderson understood the loneliness of being different. What was it that helped him discover he was more than what others perceived?

It's at the end of the story when two beautiful swans approach him on the pond that the ugly duckling discovers his real identify. Perhaps Jesus' mission was to reveal what we are to be. No one is an ugly duckling. I may feel ugly at times, but I was born a swan.

Pause for reflection: Is it difficult to see myself as a swan? Am I able to look for what is real in others? What does it mean to be "a child of God"?

The Gift of Kara

It is the heart that sees more than the mind.

John Burroughs, *Riverby*

Kara is a gothic word meaning to grieve or suffer with another person. It's close to the word *compassion* in the New Testament. Kara begins deep within ourselves as we experience the suffering of another person.

The gift of kara should be the function of spiritual leaders and is a concept in all the world religions. Unfortunately, it is often forgotten and unpracticed.

I'm reminded of the WWII story of the triage system in sorting out the wounded. It was up to doctors to color tag the wounded and dying. One color meant the case was hopeless; another that the person would live with or without help; and the third, the soldier had a chance if attended to.

Lou received a hopeless tag, but the nurse who attended Lou discovered they were from the same state and changed Lou's tag. Lou recovered.

Kara requires me to get to know another person before making a final judgment. Changing the tag is often risky. The Good Samaritan takes a chance when he helps the man lying in the ditch. The gift of kara drew him to the man. Those who passed by on the other side knew about the gift, but did not practice it.

Pause for reflection: How difficult is it for me to move beyond appearances when meeting a stranger? When have I changed my mind about another person? When did I last experience the gift of compassion?

Being Mary and Martha

She had a sister named Mary, who sat at the Lord's feet and listened to what he was saying. But Martha was distracted by her many tasks...

Luke 10:38-42

I am pulled between daily tasks and time for myself. The Mary and Martha story has almost always been used to call us to a deeper devotional life. Mary is the great spiritual example, sitting at Jesus' feet. Martha seems a little less faithful, busy in the kitchen, taking care of her guests. Listeners are called to do the one thing needful.

More than one person has said to me, "If we were all Mary's we would starve." Lessons in scripture, including parables, often focus our attention in one direction to make a point. I've come to a new understanding of the Mary and Martha story.

We are both Mary and Martha. We need quiet time alone to refresh ourselves spiritually. We must also spend time feeding our families and taking care of others. Mary and Martha together represent real life. Our task is to be responsible in both ways. This was brought home to me in the pastor's wife I knew as a high school student. She was always busy in the kitchen, but also a deeply spiritual person.

Pause for reflection: Who do I identify with most, Mary or Martha? How might I find more balance in my life? Do I know a Mary and a Martha?

Fishing Without Hooks

Attend to the grand allowing!

Martha Bartholomew

Loren Eiseley wrote a poem entitled, Gravely Then, about Edward Thomas on his way to war.

Edward Thomas, a young poet, lived near his friend of Robert Frost in England. The poem begins . . .

> Gravely then, for he was a grave man, Edward Thomas rose and taking the boy by the hand they walked to an old pool in a copse of trees . . .

The poem describes how Thomas forgot the hooks and explained to the boy that sometimes the best fishing was without hooks.

Thomas understood the need to sit and reflect on important things. On that particular day Eiseley reminds us, Edward Thomas was on his way to war.

Sadly, Thomas was killed in the war and left only a few poems behind. The poem intrigues me because of its subtle invitation to sit quietly and reflect upon what is really important, to do what Martha Bartholomew suggests and attend to the grand allowing! I'm drawn to people like Edward Thomas who fish without hooks.

I shouldn't have to wait for war or other crisis to see that every day is worthy of sitting quietly to reflect upon it. I need to give myself permission for the *grand allowing.*

Pause for reflection: When did I last sit quietly to think? Do I think sitting still without purpose is a waste of time? What keeps me from taking time for myself?

99

Time: Secular and Sacred

In our culture time can seem like an enemy, it chews us up and spits us out with appalling ease.

Kathleen Norris

Time demands our attention. "Am I on time?" "Am I late?" Tasks and obligations demand that I know the time of day.

There was a period in history when days were regulated by natural rhythms. Farmers rose with the sun and quit work at sundown. Before electric lights families went to bed early and rose early. It was a different "time."

On my visits to farms I've slipped easily into their schedules. Time is provided during the harvest for a break in the morning. At noon they eat the big meal in the kitchen before the long afternoon of work. Time is ordered by the seasons, weather, and country lifestyle.

Prayer can be such a regulatory factor. The rabbis gave their disciples an identifying prayer to pray during the day. John the Baptist gave one to his followers. Jesus gave his disciples the Lord's Prayer. I picture them taking time out to sit and listen. Did Jesus give them the prayer as a discipline to break up the time? Certainly that was how the early church saw it when they repeated the prayer at regular intervals during the day.

Pause for reflection: How dependent am I on clocks and watches? What pattern might I build into my day as a reminder to take time out? How aware am I of the natural rhythms in my life?

100

To Grow or Not to Grow?

"You've no right to grow here," said the Dormouse.
"Don't talk nonsense," said Alice more boldly.
"You know you're growing too."
"Yes, but I grow at reasonable pace," said the Dormouse,
"not in that ridiculous fashion."

Lewis Carroll, *Alice's Adventures in Wonderland*

Alice grew in an unreasonable fashion when she drank the liquid. It wasn't growth in understanding. She simply grew too large. Bigger is better and more is wanted, we tell ourselves. But is it true? Is growing excessively unfair to others? The Dormouse seemed to think so.

The Quaker author, Richard Foster, writes, "The idea of unlimited growth and expansion is deeply bedded in the American psyche." William Ophuls says, "Growth is the secular religion of American society."

It brings us back to the parable of the rich man who built many barns only to find out that his soul was required of him that very night. "What is enough?" asks E.F. Schumacher in his book, *Small is Beautiful*. How big a house do I need? How large a recreational vehicle? How much stuff — records, books, keepsakes — should I have before the Dormouse whispers: "You've no right to grow here." The answers are personal and must be decided by each of us.

I like Henry David Thoreau's recommendation. "Keep your accounts on your thumb nail."

Pause for reflection: Have I been responsible in my choices? If I had it to do it over again would I think differently? How much of my life is about my own happiness?

BookWilde Children's Books Plus

All Gene G. Bradbury books are available
through the author's website:
genegbradbury.com;
and through Amazon.com, Createspace.com,
and other retail outlets.

Other Books by Gene G. Bradbury

FACES FROM A BROKEN STAR,
Short Stories

There was a time when traveling across country one might pull into any small town in America and find a mom and pop cafe. It was a good place to order a fried chicken dinner. Farmers gathered there to compare crop prices and check the weather before working in the field. The local café has disappeared. In these stories you're invited to meet the regulars at the Broken Star Cafe. Some of the characters may sound familiar. Others who will make you laugh and cry.

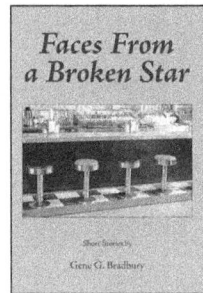

TRAVELING IN COMPANY

We never travel on our journey alone, but are linked by birth to others. They have walked before us and we follow in their footsteps. Those we come to know best on our travels we call family. From them we learn how to live. Others we meet along the way may lead us to quiet paths of reflection and spiritual practice. In this book of poems the author invites us to look at the many ways we are influenced by others as we travel together.

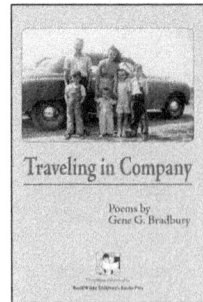

QUIET PLACES, MORNING WALKS:
Notes Between Secular and Sacred

In this book of poetry the author invites the reader to find time each day for quiet and reflection. Each poem is a poetic response to a Psalm verse. The Psalm itself is rewritten in haiku. The book of poetry is prefaced with *morning litanies* to begin the day. The book ends with *evening songs* to end the day. The collection of verse can be used in the morning or evening as a time of quiet and devotion.

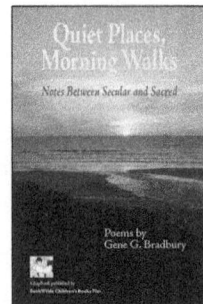

SAUNTERING WITH THOREAU

These poems begin with the author's love of Henry David Thoreau's Journals. Each poem is a reflection on a single quote by Thoreau. The poetry is a brief walk with the nineteenth century naturalist through the woods and along the rivers of Concord. Each poem invites the reader to look intently at the things around them and appreciate the place where they live. In Thoreau's words we are invited to find the kernel of life and not just the husk.

WALKING ON WATER

Walking on Water is the fourth book of poetry by author Gene G. Bradbury.

"I consider the idea of 'walking on water' a metaphor for having enough faith in oneself to risk the first step. If I'm wrong and 'walking on water' is more than metaphor, it must take great skill. To attempt the feat is to believe that more is possible. It's an invitation to pay better attention, listen more intently, see more clearly. Being human we do not have all the tools, but we can learn to pay better attention to the world around us. We can dream. We can listen to the rivers and oceans. We can give thanks for the people we know. We can listen to the sounds of nature. We can listen to the stories of others. We can send healing winds through the lives of friends and family. These poems are my own way of stepping into wakefulness. Each poem is a step onto an uncertain surface, a few moments to walk on water."

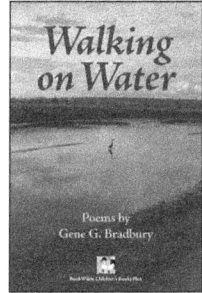

BookWilde Children's Books

Children's Books by the Author

THE MOUSE WITH WHEELS IN HIS HEAD

Meet Fergus who wants to be the first mouse to ride the new Ferris Wheel at the World's Fair. Can a tiny mouse find a way to hitch a ride without being discovered? Follow Fergus's adventure at the 1893 Chicago Exhibition.

THE MOUSE WHO WANTED TO FLY

Adventure is in Fergus's blood. His success in riding the Ferris Wheel is in the past. When Fergus learns that two brothers, Orville and Wilbur, are going to fly the first powered airplane, Fergus is eager for a new adventure. Is it possible that a mouse can be on the first flight at Kitty Hawk?

FERGUS OF LIGHTHOUSE ISLAND

Fergus, unlike his great uncle, isn't brave at all. He isn't looking for adventure. But when a hurricane threatens Lighthouse Island, adventure finds him. What will Fergus decide when the hurricane threatens the residents of Mouse Village? It's no place for a mouse who is afraid.

MISCHIEVOUS MAX, A TEDDY BEAR STORY

In Leon's room you will find many teddy bears. Most of them are soft and wonderful to take to bed. But there is one bear who Leon never takes to bed. His name is Max Bear and his fur tickles and his eyes are beastly. Leon knows something else about Max Bear. What if Leon tries sleeping with Max Bear for just one night? Would that be so bad? Leon is about to find out.

The above books are illustrated by Victoria Wickell-Stewart
and are available through the author's website: genegbradbury.com;
and through Amazon.com, Createspace.com, and other retail outlets.

CLOUD CLIMBER

What were his parents thinking, leaving him for three boring weeks at his grandparent's farm? There would be no internet or cable television and what was worse, only Cousin Emily for company. But on a trip to town with his grandfather, Seth learns of Three Friends Hill and the Banshee's Cave. Are these linked to the discovery of a giant kite Seth and Emily find in the old barn? The three weeks literally fly past and the cousins find that Boring Farm is not so boring after all.

All Gene G. Bradbury books are available
through the author's website:
genegbradbury.com;
and through Amazon.com, Createspace.com,
and other retail outlets.